The Scots Philosophical Monograph Series

While this monograph series is published on behalf of the Scots Philosophical Club, refereed by a panel of distinguished philosophers in the Club, and has as one of its aims the provision of a publishing outlet for philosophical work being done in Scotland, it is nevertheless international. The Club hopes to bring out original works, written in a lively and readable style, and devoted to central areas of current philosophical concern, from philosophers working anywhere in the world.

As a deliberate policy we have specified no areas of the subject on which the series is to concentrate. The emphasis is on originality rather than, say, on surveys of literature, commentaries on the work of others, or exegesis. Historical works will be included only in so far as they also contribute significantly to topical debates.

As well as our debt to the referees and consulting editors, we have to acknowledge a very real debt to the universities of Glasgow, Edinburgh, Aberdeen, Stirling and St Andrews who—despite the current stringencies—have given financial support to the series.

Series Editors: Andrew Brennan, William Lyons

Consulting Editors:
J R Cameron *Aberdeen*
Neil Cooper *Dundee*
Robin Downie *Glasgow*
R W Hepburn *Edinburgh*
Bernard Mayo *St Andrews*
Neil Tennant *Stirling*
A G Wernham *Aberdeen*
Crispin Wright *St Andrews*

Scots Philosophical Monographs Number Four

HISTORICAL EXPLANATION RECONSIDERED

Scots Philosophical Monographs

Scots Philosophical Monographs Number Four

HISTORICAL EXPLANATION RECONSIDERED

GORDON GRAHAM

Series Editors Andrew Brennan & William Lyons

ABERDEEN UNIVERSITY PRESS

First published 1983
Aberdeen University Press
A member of the Pergamon Group

© Gordon Graham 1983

British Library Cataloguing in Publication Data
Graham, Gordon
Historical explanation reconsidered. — (Scots
philosophical monographs ISSN 0144-3063; 4)
1. History — Philosophy
I. Title   II. Series
901   D16.8
ISBN 0 08 028478 7

PRINTED IN GREAT BRITAIN AT
ABERDEEN UNIVERSITY PRESS

Contents

Preface

This monograph sets out to examine the course taken by a great deal of discussion in the philosophy of history since the publication of the essays 'Historical Explanation' by Morton White in 1942 and 'The Function of General Laws in History' by Carl Hempel in the following year. Its central contention is that the subject of historical explanation has been confused by uncertainty over the relation between philosophy and its objects, a confusion which may be dispelled fairly easily. The result of dispelling it, however, is to show that explanations which may properly be called historical do not present any great philosophical difficulty or complexity and that two dichotomies, which have been the source of a lot of disagreement, those between history and nature and historical and scientific explanation, are false.

Most of this essay was written at the University of Minnesota. I am grateful to members of the Department of Philosophy in Minneapolis and to the Center for the Philosophy of Science both for their hospitality and for their discussion of my chosen topic of research. In particular I owe to these discussions the objections considered in Chapter 5. I am also indebted to my colleague Mr C J Bryant for copious comments and criticisms.

My visit to Minnesota was partly funded by the British Academy and by the Heinz and Anna Kroch Foundation, whose support I gladly acknowledge.

1

'X' and the philosophy of 'X'

It is generally agreed amongst philosophers, and perhaps a wider circle of opinion, that philosophy is not an empirical inquiry. Nevertheless it is not without its objects of study—knowledge, morality, God, existence and so on. In many of these cases it is at least arguable that the sense of 'object' here is radically different from the sense in which that atom or distant galaxies are the objects of a scientist's inquiry. But in other cases, especially where an empirical inquiry with exactly the same object (or so it appears) is familiar to us, a question arises about the relation of philosophy to its object. This is most evident, perhaps, in the context of the interest twentieth-century philosophers have taken in the character of other disciplines—history, science and social science chiefly—which have also been the subject of strictly empirical studies, namely history and sociology. If philosophy is not empirical how does it stand in relation to these? In other words, what is the connection between what philosophers say about history or science and what historians and scientists do?

According to some philosophers the relation is primarily critical and normative; according to others, though it is not empirical, it is in the last analysis descriptive. On the first view the job of the philosopher is to construct a coherent conception of history or of science on the basis of abstract argument and in the context of a systematic treatment of human knowledge as a whole. His concern is with appearance and reality, his enterprise informed by a desire to discriminate between the apparently and the really scientific, the speciously and the truly historical. This way of proceeding is best exemplified in some of the later idealist philosophers, notably the Collingwood of *Speculum Mentis* and Oakeshott in *Experience and its Modes*. In the former Collingwood treats of art, religion, science, history and philosophy itself; in the latter Oakeshott

1

distinguishes science, history and practice, has something to say about philosophy, and has added an account of art in the essay 'The Voice of Poetry in the Conversation of Mankind'. Neither of these writers would claim to have given accounts of these varieties of human knowledge that are totally independent of the study of history or science as we encounter them in daily life but their arguments have an air of essentialism and abstraction that philosophers of another tradition have been anxious to avoid. For it is at least part of the self-image of so-called analytical philosophy that its business is mere description and that it makes no attempt to establish criteria for the truly scientific or truly historical, but simply sets out the character of history and science as it finds them. A quite general version of this doctrine is to be found in Wittgenstein's *Investigations* where it is said that 'Philosophy may in no way interfere with the actual use of language; it can in the end only describe it . . . it leaves everything as it is' (41: para 124)*. No doubt this is the source of much of its prevalence and popularity elsewhere but it has also been stated with explicit reference to the narrower fields of the philosophy of history and the philosophy of science and by those whose indebtedness to Wittgenstein is less than certain. For example, Kuhn, in his famous book *The Structure of Scientific Revolutions*, records that his own dissatisfaction with existing theories of science had this origin, saying, 'Those conceptions [of the nature of science] whatever their pedagogic utility and their abstract plausibility . . . did not at all fit the enterprise that historical study displayed' (30: p. vii). And he asks in general 'How could history of science fail to be a source of phenomena to which theories about knowledge may legitimately be asked to apply?' (30: p. 9). Similarly, in his preface to *The Nature of Historical Explanation* Patrick Gardiner espouses the descriptive method for the reason that 'By trying to keep the actual practice of historians constantly in view we may at least be able to see some of the disputes that have raged concerning the "philosophy of history" in a truer perspective' (25: p. xii).

It should not be supposed, however, that the difference is straightforwardly one between modern analytical philosophy and old-fashioned Idealism. Popper's philosophy of science, which in being positivist is anti-idealist, is nonetheless intended to provide us with the means of distinguishing between science and pseudo-science; while Oakeshott, whatever the actual character of his arguments, and contrary to their appearance, holds that philosophical reflection is parasitic upon its objects, accepting as he does Hegel's dictum that the owl of Minerva takes its flight only at the dusk. In any case the question we have to deal

---

* Bibliography, p 81

with may not really amount to a difference in method such as might be thought to mark off two different schools, but a difference in the account of method philosophers have given. This is suggested by the fact that, considered in isolation, each of these conceptions of philosophical method encounters difficulties which make it doubtful if either could actually be pursued and thus whether either has been pursued.

The problem with the first, what Peirce called 'the high priori way', is that no matter how well it is done, we can (and must) ask of any construction why it is to be called 'history' or 'science' rather than some arbitrarily chosen name. Suppose that we have delineated a distinctive mode of inquiry which understands the world under the aspect of quantity (which is roughly how Oakeshott characterises science); what reason have we to call this mode of understanding *science*? The most obvious answer, one which it is hard to see how we can avoid, is that the conception is in some way a description of the practice of scientific inquiry as it has grown up, so that the actual facts about scientific inquiry must act, in the way Kuhn suggests, as a check upon our constructions. Without this, there is the constant danger that our conception of history or of science turns out to be a stipulative definition, 'a preconceived idea to which reality *must* correspond'. This, according to Wittgenstein, is a 'dogmatism into which we fall so easily in doing philosophy' (41: para 131). But if this is right, how then can our conceptions of history or science have the kind of independence which would enable us to use them in passing judgement upon various intellectual endeavours, pronouncing some of them to be science and others not? For it seems that such a pronouncement will amount to no more than the expression of a preference for one historically discoverable mode of inquiry and against another. Thus the prescriptive account of philosophy turns out to require an appeal to the facts which in turn destroys its prescriptive capacity.

A similar difficulty, surprisingly perhaps, also attends the pure description conception of philosophical method, however. If we have no prior and in some sense independent idea of science or history, upon what items in the whole range of human knowledge and inquiry are we to fix for our describing to begin? Consider, for instance, the debate about whether social science is science. If this is a philosophical question, and it is generally thought to be, and if mere description is the proper course for philosophy it would seem sufficient for the social scientist, the status of whose subject is in question, simply to describe its procedures and declare these to be the logic of science or a science, not on the basis of any affinity it bears to physics, say, but just because among all the enterprises that have gone by the name of science his is one. On this score, it is enough for the practitioners of any intellectual enterprise (astrology, for instance) to establish the scientific character of their activities by declaring them to be scientific and persuading others to do likewise.

It might be supposed that this attempt to foist the difficulties of the prescriptive method on the descriptive method results from a failure to understand it properly. The whole thrust of the idea that philosophy is descriptive, it must be said, is to urge that we should abandon the question 'What is *real* science?' and be content to describe the variety of things that fall under that label, physics, sociology, psychology. Philosophy as description aims to combat the philosophical craving for generality. But this rejoinder fails to recognise the deep-seatedness of the difficulty. To set out to describe presupposes that we can pick out what it is we are to describe. About this there is no very general difficulty, it is true. There may be an interesting problem about how we can tell historians from hawks or handsaws but this could scarcely be thought to be a problem which the proponent of the view that philosophers of history ought to pay attention to what historians actually do must solve if his view is to be creditable. There is a problem, however, when he tries to decide which bits of the historian's activity the philosopher is especially concerned with. Of course we have readily available the *form* of an answer to that question. It is easy and acceptable enough to say that the philosopher is interested in the logic of history, or perhaps the structure of history. But it remains to give some substance to these formulae. Which of the logical operations historians perform are bits of the logic of *history*? No doubt historians avoid contradicting themselves, but the observation that they do could hardly be said to tell us anything special about history. Again, historians may pass moral judgement upon the figures whose histories they write but we can still ask whether they do this in their capacity as historians (in which case their expertise counts for something) or in their capacity as moral agents (in which case it does not). In short, before we can describe the logic of history we must know what inferences, explanations and so on are peculiarly historical. And if we know this are we not then able to supply some prior and independent conception of historical (or scientific) knowledge?

It thus appears that each of the paths with which we began sooner or later leads to the other. If we insist on either as the proper method in philosophy the subject simply cannot proceed. How, then, is philosophy to be done? A familiar answer is one which urges us to abandon the whole business of setting out to give 'an account of X'. It is right, some will tell us, to think of philosophy as descriptive but wrong to think of it as some sort of descriptive *science*. Philosophy is not the discovery of new facts, but the assembly of reminders, things we already know, to a particular purpose, the purpose being the dissolution of the conceptual problem which holds our thought captive at any particular time. And this problem, whatever it is, determines what we are to describe, so that we have no need of preconceptions. The questions 'What is history?', 'What is science?', then, are not genuine philosophical problems and consequently any account of the method by which they might be answered will not constitute a coherent account of philosophical method. Rather, philosophical questions concerning history will take the form 'How is it possible to know anything about the past, when the past is dead and gone?', and the method of their solution (or more properly dissolution) will consist in reminding ourselves of cases of knowledge of the past so that the picture which prompted the puzzle is removed.

In certain branches of philosophy, it seems to me, this conception of the subject has a good deal to be said for it, but as a general account of philosophical method it encounters an important difficulty. It is a revolutionary conception, one, that is to say, which aims to alter, correct, even to reverse, the direction in which philosophy has gone at some points in its history. One result of this is that the title 'philosophy' must, strictly speaking, be denied to the works of some of its most famous practitioners, most obviously perhaps Plato, whose works abound in essentialist questions, or Hobbes and Spinoza in whose works conceptual problems of the sort here referred to are largely absent. I do not regard this, however, as a *reductio ad absurdum* of the thesis, since quite possibly it is correct. What is important in the present context is that, if this is indeed one of its implications, it can hardly avoid the very problem I have here introduced it to dissolve. Take, for instance, Collingwood's *Idea of History.*[1] In this book Collingwood self-consciously addresses the essentialist question 'What is history?' and he sets out to give an account of history in just the way that is said to be mistaken on the conception of philosophy we are examining. What he proceeds to say is full of interest and it certainly seems reasonable to think that if Collingwood is not wholly successful, his enterprise is one which we might undertake and, following his lead, aspire to do better in. Moreover his work and similar attempts to improve upon it have gone by the name 'philosophy' so that to declare them devoid of truly philosophical character seems to be judging them in the light of a conception of philosophy which ignores the facts of linguistic usage and the history of the subject. If this is true then to use Wittgenstein's conception of philosophy[2] to dissolve the descriptive/normative dispute is to employ a conception of philosophy which is itself normative. But if there can be such a conception of philosophy why

---

[1] Notes are on p 79

not of science or of history? This dissolution makes the same sort of move as it aims to rule out.

It might be replied that philosophy, unlike other subjects, not only does but must reflect upon itself and that this makes a difference. Certainly this is an interesting fact about philosophy but I do not know that it makes any difference here. For presumably, if there are criteria which any decent piece of philosophy must satisfy, these must be satisfied regardless of the subject of the philosophising. After all, there can be histories of history, but this does not suggest or imply that these are any less in need of evidence than histories of anything else.

There is a different solution from the one we have been considering which also rejects the dichotomy between prescription and description upon which the difficulty I have been discussing rests. It is wrong, on this view, for the philosopher when he looks at history, say, to suppose that he can eschew either concern with the facts or prescriptive conclusions. His business is in a sense an elucidation of the rules of a practice and in order to formulate the rules of a practice it is clearly essential to look at what the participants in that practice do. But once a rule has been formulated it carries with it implications of right and wrong. Consider drawing up rules of grammar. In order to conclude that the past participle of 'to go' is 'gone', not 'went', it is necessary to find out how people actually speak. But of course it is a necessary feature of rules that they can be broken and since some people do say 'I have went', we cannot record what participants in the practice say without discrimination. Certainly what we want to find out is how English is spoken, but what we are after is proper usage, not any and every use. Consequently the rules we formulate will be both a reflection of what people say and a criterion by which to judge what they say. In like manner philosophical thought about some concept or other must result in a general account of that concept which undoubtedly depends upon uses of that concept in contexts other than philosophy but which may also on occasion stand in judgement upon particular and even common uses.

This conception of philosophical method is to be found in Nelson Goodman's well-known views on the justification of principles of deductive logic. 'Rules and particular inferences alike are justified by being brought into agreement with each other. *A rule is amended if it yields an inference we are unwilling to accept; an inference is rejected if it violates a rule we are unwilling to amend.* The process of justification is the delicate one of making mutual adjustments between rules and accepted inferences; and in the agreement achieved lies the only justification needed for either' (27: p. 64, italics original). In a similar manner the justification of a philosophical account of history or science lies in mutual adjustment between the demand for coherence, consistency and generality on the one hand and well-entrenched identifications and commonly accepted facts about history or science on the other. Philosophy thus aims at what has elsewhere been called 'reflective equilibrium' (see 37: p. 20).

There is much to be said for this point of view. Indeed if the direction in which the argument has led us so far approaches the truth, it seems that there is no other solution available to us. If philosophy cannot be wholly descriptive, if it cannot be wholly prescriptive either, and if it cannot avoid being partly one and partly the other, the only conclusion we can draw is that the prescriptive demands of generality must be held in check by the descriptive record of matters of common agreement.

And yet it is not altogether easy to see how this conception is supposed to work in particular contexts. The method relies upon there *being* matters of common agreement but very often it is difficult to say first what such agreement is to be about and secondly how mere convergence of opinion is supposed to help. In Goodman's case it is the justification of deduction which is at issue and the agreement to which we must appeal is obviously agreement over good and bad inferences. Furthermore it does seem that when we say things like 'We just do accept inferences of this sort, or reject inferences of that sort', we are appealing to something fairly fundamental and not just to a happy coincidence of opinion. This is seen by the fact that disagreement is in some way, hard to articulate no doubt, quite implausible, so that the agreement has a certain sort of authority. Thus there has to be, as there is, something far-fetched about the doubt whether from the facts that all men are mortal and Socrates is a man, we can conclude that Socrates is mortal. But once we leave the realms of deductive logic, the subject of agreement and its authority are very much harder to detect.

Let us return, for instance, to the philosophy of history and more specifically to the topic of this monograph, historical explanation. The philosopher wants to give an account of historical explanation which will have sufficient generality to enable us to pick out a class of explanations in a way which shows them to be, in some sense or other, of a kind. His account must be general, consistent and coherent certainly, but with what, on the model of reflective equilibrium, is it also supposed to agree? The only obvious candidate is the identification of historical explanations in non-philosophical circles, amongst historians themselves perhaps. But here the difficulties begin, for we will find, I think, first that the term 'historical explanation' has no great currency outside philosophy and secondly that amongst historians who have anything to say on the matter there is no very extensive agreement. Worse still, even if there were, there is no reason to think that this would be any more than mere convergence of opinion, because there is nothing very odd or far-fetched (as I hope to show) about the insistence of some philosophers that the explanations historians give and accept are not, properly speaking, explanations at all. Let me underline this point. I am not saying that these philosophers are not wrong, rather that whether they are or not is something we might sensibly discuss, whereas we cannot sensibly discuss the validity of the inference about Socrates. We must just accept that this is an instance of a valid inference and that such arguments are given and accepted as good ones.

Historical explanation, however, is only one context. In fact I should claim that there are many occasions upon which similar problems arise so that though the aim of reflective equilibrium may be reasonable enough as an abstract account of the relation of philosophy to its objects, it is not easy to adopt it as a method. More particularly, for my purposes it is unable to establish any clear connection between philosophical argument about history, and the practice of the study of history. In this it is not alone, of course, for we have now seen that none of the four conceptions of philosophy we have examined will do this satisfactorily. Indeed it is part of the purpose of this monograph to introduce a fifth just in order to solve some problems about historical explanation. It is however, a method with more general application than this for in a number of contexts I think it quite possible to find a basic proposition that will relate any subsequent philosophical argument which begins with it to its object, i.e. that aspect of human experience in which we are interested, in a clear and obvious way. If the proposition is to be genuinely basic, that is if it is to lend the argument which depends upon it any special weight, it will need to be incontrovertible at least in something of the same way in which the cases of inferring to which Goodman appeals are incontrovertible. This might be accomplished by making the basic proposition state something rather obvious, or at least something which no one interested in the subject would seriously want to deny, or by making it a necessary truth. My own view is that propositions of the first sort are rather more desirable since about necessary truths there can be a great deal of dispute, but the point I want to make is that from such a proposition we may be able to draw out implications sufficient to form a more general conception of history, art, science or whatever it may be. If we can and if we can use this conception to uncover inconsistencies in our thought and to challenge and rectify the claims of other theorists, we shall have an understanding of the sort philosophers typically seek, and one, moreover, which can hardly be accused of stipulation or vacuity since it rests upon a claim about the object in question which no one is going to deny.

An example might be this: the study of history is investigation into what happened in the past. This claim is basic in the sense both that it is minimal, for many philosophers and historians will wish to claim that history is much more than this, and that it is pretty well beyond dispute, since we shall all agree that, whatever else it might be, the study of history is at least an investigation into what happened in the past. Yet, despite its basic character, it can be shown, though it is not my business to do so here, that this characterisation has sufficiently important implications for us to form a conception of history with which to challenge, even to refute, a good deal that philosophers and historians have written about it.

My abstract description of the method and this gesture towards an example does very little, I realise, to establish that on any given occasion we could proceed in this manner with much hope of success. It is not my intention, however, to elaborate a general conception of philosophy which might solve the problems about philosophical method I have been discussing, but to find a way of exposing and resolving certain confusions and difficulties which are to be found in the philosophical literature on historical explanation. Nevertheless, the main part of the argument will have added interest, I hope, by illustrating how any 'Philosophy of X' might usefully be pursued.

In the next three chapters I shall try to establish that uncertainty about the proper role of appeals to the practice of historians and the pages of history books has vitiated a good deal of the debate about historical explanation, and in succeeding sections I attempt to remedy this by the introduction of a basic proposition of the sort I have just described.

2

How is 'explanation' to be qualified?

Anyone who peruses the philosophical literature on explanation must come away impressed and perplexed by the seemingly endless ways in which 'explanation' can be qualified. Without undertaking an exhaustive survey I have compiled the following formidable list:

aesthetic, biological, causal, chemical, deductive-nomological, dispositional, functional, genetic, geographical, historical, ideological, inductive, mechanical, physical, probabilistic, psychological, rational, scientific, sociological, statistical, technical and teleological.

Some of these terms are, no doubt, intended to convey the same meaning (like 'probabilistic' and 'statistical'), but even if we discount equivalents we still have a very large number. What is more I should not claim to have included in the list all those qualifications that have ever been employed but only those that it is easy to find occurring in the work of more than one writer.

In the face of this variety we may reasonably ask what it is that qualifications of explanation are supposed to do. A natural answer is that each qualification is supposed to pick out a distinctive kind of explanation. This suggestion however, presents us with two difficulties. First, it is quite unclear in what respect explanations of different kinds are different. Compare, for example, the classification of dwellings. Dwellings maybe have a host of different predicates applied to them but it is possible to arrange these predicates into groups—for instance, detached, semi-detached, flatted, single-storeyed—such that it is easy to specify the respect in which each is different, in this case design. Now what counterpart is there to design in the case of explanation? 'Structure' and 'logic' are familiar candidates but the longer one looks at them the less clear it is *exactly* what the structure or logic of an explanation is supposed to be. Indeed I am inclined to think that these words are simply ways of referring to rather than elucidating what it is the philosopher means to talk about here. The position is further complicated, in any case, by a second difficulty. The predicates by which we find explanation qualified and which I have listed do not appear to compete in the same categories. That is to say not all of them are incommensurable. Chemical, biological and physical explanations, for instance, are also said to be scientific, and historical explanations are often said to be rational. About the compatibility or incompatibility of others there is some dispute and those familiar with the literature in this area will be aware of interminable debates over whether historical explanations are also scientific and whether rational explanations are or can also be causal. Now in so far as the same explanation can be classified under two different labels we cannot say that the labels can mark off different kinds of explanation, and in so far as there is uncertainty about whether this is possible or not, we shall have to suspend judgement on the question. Given, however, that in order to conduct such debates we must be able to use the qualifications over which the dispute arises, it follows that if there is to be any rationale for the use of the different terms it must reside in something other than our grasp of where the lines between different kinds of explanation are to be drawn. In other words, any principles we may be able to formulate which could govern the ways in which explanation is to be qualified, will not amount to the distinction of different kinds of explanation.

The importance of this observation is easy to demonstrate. Most discussions of explanation in history and the social sciences have turned around whether explanation is the same here as it is in the natural sciences. This question has usually been answered by the introduction of certain distinctions, like that between rational and causal explanation. But plainly, this settles any argument about the sameness or difference of explanation in history and the social sciences only if we are clear about whether and in what respect rational and causal explanations are different. And this, I am claiming, is just what we are not clear about.

It seems then, that before we can launch into a discussion of, say, historical explanation, we must prepare the ground by making clear what we are doing when we qualify the term 'explanation' in one way rather than another. This point has gone almost unnoticed, and in consequence a good deal of philosophising on the subject has been confounded. But it has not gone altogether unnoticed. Indeed in his celebrated essay 'Historical Explanation' Morton White centres his discussion around the observation that 'the problem of analysing historical explanation is connected with the general problem of analysing what it means to say that explanation is of a certain sort' (16: p. 212). He takes the view that in all the expressions in which it is normally used 'explanation' has the same meaning and what is more has the well-known Hempelian form. The basis for any qualification of the term, therefore, cannot have to do with logical structure and White advances the thesis that 'the determination of the type of an explanation depends on the terms that appear in it' (16: p. 229). Thus physical explanations are so called because they employ terms peculiar to the science of physics, biological explanations because they employ the terms of biology, and so on.

White has here provided us with a principle of classification that is plausible and easy to state clearly. To that degree he has overcome the difficulties which the variety of qualifications presents. For in its light we can discern what each qualification means and, just as importantly, whether explanation can actually be qualified in the way that some writers have said it can. Unfortunately, however, the principle he offers us is not a satisfactory one. In the first place, despite the title of the essay, White is forced to conclude that since there do not seem to be any terms peculiar to historical study there does not seem to be any reason to distinguish peculiarly *historical* explanations. It is true that he does not exclude the possibility of discovering peculiarly historical terms, but he holds that anything we might come up with could only artificially be distinguished from sociology, so that the hope of marking off historical explanations from all others seems a false one. This is an unfortunate conclusion for someone whose aim is to tell us about *historical* explanation, but of course this does not show that what he says is incorrect. However, as I hope the remainder of this essay will demonstrate, since there really is a class of explanations which we have reason to call historical, any principle which gives us this result must be erroneous.

In the second place, the plausibility of White's principle is diminished considerably once we leave the relatively straightforward cases of physics, chemistry, and biology, which are so plainly subjects with terms peculiar to them. White offers the examples of psychology and sociology but, even ignoring the fact that what appears to be a specialised vocabulary sometimes turns out to be nothing but jargon, neither of these subjects has the stability or unity which would enable us to say with certainty which terms are peculiar to them. More importantly, however, there are many qualifications in the list—like causal, rational, probabilistic, functional—which do not refer to any specialised science at all and whose meaning therefore cannot be accommodated by White's principle. A hardened defender of the thesis might claim of course that for just this reason we ought not to use these qualifications but this seems an illegitimate move and in any case it is contrary to White's argument because he supports his principle with the claim that this is in fact the way in which we do determine which are different kinds of explanation.

Thirdly, in some cases at least analysis of familiar qualifications in terms of White's principle seems to produce results at odds with what we normally mean. For instance, 'statistical explanation' does not normally mean 'explanation in terms peculiar to statistics' and 'genetic explanation', which at least one writer holds to be common in history, does not mean 'explanation in the terms peculiar to the science of genetics'.

Fourthly, the principle only gets going because White supposes that the form of explanation is everywhere the same. In the essay I am discussing he does not advance much argument in support of this view (though he does elsewhere) and clearly if he is wrong on this point there must be a distinction or range of distinctions to be made which his principle cannot encompass. In fact, after White's essay was published Hempel recognised the need to introduce a distinction between deductive-nomological and probabilistic explanations and this is just such a distinction.

This final objection suggests that it may not be White's principle which is unsatisfactory so much as the attempt to arrive at any single and quite general principle of classification that will cover and elucidate all the qualifications we have occasion to employ. If one range of distinctions—physical, chemical, biological—differentiates according to the terms employed and another range—deductive, inductive—according to logical form, and other ranges according to other features perhaps, then there is no reason to think that there is any general system of classification or distinction to be found. The lesson to be learnt from this, I think, is that philosophers who wish to employ terms from or add to the baffling list of qualifications to be found in the literature on explanation should not be required to produce a general principle of classification but obey some other constraint, like a rule of method. One such simple constraint would be this. We need not set any general limits to the number of qualifications a philosopher can reasonably employ, so long as he makes it clear what he means when he qualifies the term 'explanation' in the way he does.

Though this rule takes us in the right direction, as it stands it will not do. A writer must tell us not only what he means by a qualification but what the point of qualifying explanation in this way is. Moreover, for philosophy at least, it is not enough that the point have something to do with his personal interests or desires. It must have something to do with its being explanation that is qualified. For example, someone might set about classifying explanations according to whether they were long or short and even define 'long' and 'short' quite precisely by stipulating word lengths. In this case we cannot be uncertain as to his meaning and he might tell us that the point of his distinction lies in his wish to find out if in general long explanations need to be as long as they are. This is a legitimate exercise (having to do with stylistics perhaps), if a somewhat odd one, but it has no philosophical interest because plainly the length of an explanation is quite incidental to its being an explanation (though not, presumably, to its being the explanation it is).

The requirement that the meaning and point of each qualification be made clear is not strict enough, therefore. In addition we must insist that the qualification have something to do with its being explanation that is qualified. Such a requirement is unlikely to meet with much opposition first because it seems to constitute an eminently reasonable demand and secondly because it is a very mild one. On its own, however, it would not I think, get us very far in the business of clarifying the debates about explanation in which so many of these qualifications have appeared. We must also require some reason to call explanations of the kind distinguished by this rather than some other name. In other words, we must try to do what White's principle attempted to do without the rigidity which it involved, that is, leaving open the possibility not only of different qualifications but qualifications according to different aspects. I do not propose to produce any further argument in favour of this second requirement which is in any case another very mild one, because I hope that the rest of the monograph will justify its introduction, but it may be useful to offer a couple of illustrations of qualifications which meet it. For example, 'rational' when applied to explanation, at least in some of its uses, meets both requirements. If rational explanations are defined as 'explanations in terms of reasons', to call an explanation a rational one tells us something about it as an explanation, viz. that the *explanans* consists of reasons, and makes it plain, self-evident in fact, why it is called 'rational'. Again, an explanation might be described as 'statistical' if it consists in showing the statistical relevance of *explanans* to *explanandum* and on this definition 'statistical' would also satisfy the requirements I have laid down.

We have, then, two very general rules for the qualification of explanation.

(1)   Any qualification must have something to do with its being explanation that is qualified.

(2)   There must be some reason given as to why the explanations so qualified should be called by this rather than any other name.

So general and so vague are these requirements that they are unlikely to be disputed. Indeed it may appear that they will produce only trivial definitions and be ridiculously easy to meet. In a sense both points are sound but the aim of this essay is to show that in the case of historical explanation though both conditions can be satisfied with the greatest of ease they never have been and that this failure has led the discussion of historical explanation badly astray.

3

The Covering Law theory and its opponents

It is a mark of the astonishing impact of the work of Carl Hempel in the philosophy of history that since the publication of his famous essay 'The Function of General Laws in History' in 1942, almost the whole of the literature on historical explanation has consisted in the discussion of whether he is right or wrong. Even philosophers who have arrived at conclusions radically at odds with Hempel's have taken his theory as their starting point. And this is testimony both to the simplicity with which he presents it and to its enormous appeal. It is not my purpose to add to the discussion of its merits here. In fact I want to claim that the real issues concerning historical explanation do not turn upon the adequacy or inadequacy of Hempel's theory and that close attention to the debate between Hempel and his opponents shows this.

It is necessary to begin with an outline of Hempel's thesis but there is no need to attempt a summary for Hempel has provided us with one which could hardly be improved upon. His view is that

[an] explanatory account may be regarded as an argument to the effect that the event to be explained (let me call it the *explanandum* event) was to be expected by reason of certain explanatory facts. These may be divided into two groups: (1) particular facts and (2) uniformities expressed by general laws. . . . The kind of explanation thus characterized I will call deductive-nomological explanation; for it amounts to a deductive subsumption of the *explanandum* under principles which have the character of general laws; it answers the question '*Why* did the *explanandum* event occur?' . . .

Now let me turn to the second basic type of scientific explanation. This kind of explanation, too, is nomological, i.e. it accounts for a given phenomenon by reference to general laws or theoretical principles; but some or all of these are of probabilistic-statistical form i.e. they are, generally speaking, assertions to the effect that if certain specified conditions are realized, then an occurrence of such and such a kind will come about with such and such a statistical probability (9: pp. 10–13).

Hempel, as is well known, believes that these models are applicable to the social as well as the natural sciences and especially that they apply to explanation in history. It is an important part of his view that 'Our two schemata exhibit, I think, one important aspect of the methodological unity of all empirical science' (9: p. 32) and that 'it is unwarranted and futile to attempt the demarcation of sharp boundary lines between the different fields of scientific research, and an autonomous development of each of the fields' (28: p. 243).

Objections to the covering law theory[3] are legion and it would be a tedious business to review them all, but since my interest is only in Hempel's contribution to the philosophy of history it will be sufficient, as I hope to show, to treat them in a general way. The objections are largely of two sorts. First, some philosophers have claimed to find internal inconsistencies in Hempel's elaboration of the theory. For instance, Michael Scriven argues that Hempel's 'logical argument for correlation of good predictions with good explanations is not formally sound' (15: p. 45). I shall not be concerned with objections like this since they have nothing in particular to do with the applicability of the models to history. The second sort of objection takes the form of counterexamples but here again we may distinguish between two sorts. First there are counterexamples which refer us to the business of explaining things in general and secondly there are those that refer us to explanations in history. W C Salmon has devised one of the first sort, a counterexample to the statistical or probabilistic schema:

> John Jones was almost certain to recover from his cold within a week because he took vitamin C, and almost all those colds clear up within a week after the administration of vitamin C.

Although this argument corresponds exactly to Hempel's inductive model it fails to explain because colds tend to clear up within a week regardless of the medication administered, and though the argument is valid and the premises true, commonsense tells us that it is a pretty poor advertisement for vitamin C. Salmon also has a counterexample to the deductive model, which he takes from Kyburg:

> This sample of table salt dissolves in water because it has had a dissolving spell cast upon it, and all samples of table salt that have had dissolving spells cast upon them dissolve in water (38: p. 33).

Again the premises are true and the argument valid but we know that salt dissolves in water regardless of spells, and that this coincidence with Hempel's model is not going to convince us of the scientific respectability of magic.

A third example, which comes from Bromberger, is instanced by Hempel himself.

Suppose that a flagpole stands vertically on level ground and subtends an angle of 45 degrees when viewed from the ground level at a distance of 80 feet. This information, in conjunction with some elementary theorems of geometry, implies deductively that the pole is 80 feet high. The theorems in question must here be understood as belonging to physical geometry and thus as having the status of general laws, or better, general theoretical principles of physics. Hence the deductive is of the type (2.1) [i.e. deductive-nomological]. And yet we would not say that its premises *explained* the fact that the pole is 80 feet high, in the sense of showing why it is that the pole has a height of 80 feet (8: p. 109).

Not all of these counterexamples may be good ones. It has been suggested for instance that the major premise in Kyburg's salt-dissolving case is not genuinely law-like and the 'explanation' not therefore an instance of Hempel's model, and Hempel, in the essay from which I have just quoted, thinks he has a way round Bromberger's. But we need not examine their force closely here because the point I want to make about them concerns an assumption that all of them make and which must hold good for any examples of this sort. It is that we have some unreflective grasp on the notion of explanation, one independent of any account we may offer or be offered, and that this grasp is of a kind good enough to enable us to reject accounts of explanation which conflict with it. If this were not so, if, say, what we call or refuse to call explanation is a matter of choice or mere opinion, the business of producing counterexamples of the sort just illustrated must be quite worthless. This is not to say that our linguistic intuitions are infallible, since on occasion we may see reason to overrule them, but that at least sometimes the attempt to reject or revise them must be rather obviously contrived or far-fetched.

Counterexamples of the second sort are those taken from history books. Dray argues that 'the explanation of human behaviour as it is usually given in history books has features which make the covering law model peculiarly inept' (23: p. 432), and Donagan sets out a number of illustrations of this.

Mr J. A. Williamson in his excellent short history, *The Evolution of England*, explains the Scandinavian invasion of Britain in the first half of the ninth century thus: 'The Norsemen and Danes who sailed south to the Irish Sea and to the shores of the English Channel were plunderers first and settlers by an afterthought. Like the early Anglo-Saxons, they came to sack a civilised land, and only when they had stolen all they could get did they think of occupying its soil' (pp. 47–48). If any buried assumption is to be resuscitated from this it would be, I suppose, that all men, or all Norsemen and Danes, and perhaps Anglo-Saxons too, are plunderers first and settlers by afterthought. Plausible this assumption may be, but it would be fantastic to suppose that Williamson would consider his explanation weakened if exceptions could be found to it. Mr J. N. L. Myers' explanation of the Saxon invasions in the fifth and sixth centuries (vol. 1 of the *Oxford History of England*, pp. 339–351), though too long to quote, also resembles Hempel's example [of an explanation that is incomplete]. Now, it is plain that both Williamson and Myers consider their explanations true, and both cite evidence which is convincing to an amateur. It is equally clear that they do not consider them imperfect, or mere sketches. They are not final, because further questions must be asked. But to the question, Why did those groups of Norsemen and Danes sail south? Williamson professes to have given an historically perfect, though corrigible, answer. Myers implicitly makes a similar claim.

The Hempelian theory, therefore, contradicts at least some good historians' opinions about their explanations (5: pp. 432–3).

As in this case, counterexamples of the second sort aim to show, not that Hempel has got explanation wrong, but that he has got *historical* explanation wrong. Hempel takes criticisms of this sort very seriously and expends considerable effort in replying to them. Yet if he means what he says, there is no way in which he *could* misrepresent history and all objections of this second sort must be beside the point. The reason for this may be brought out in the following way.

According to Hempel all explanation is of two sorts, neither of which is to be called historical explanation. Suppose he is right. Then, if anything in history is explanation, it must be deductive or statistical; if it is not, then whatever it is and however valuable in the writing of history books, it cannot be explanation. Conversely, suppose he is wrong. Since neither of the schemata he outlines is to be called historical explanation, he cannot be wrong because *historical* explanation is not as he says it is, but because explanation is not as he says it is. Either way the Hempelian models cannot misrepresent history or historical explanation. Therefore, if we can produce a convincing counterexample its coming from the pages of a history book will be quite incidental to its being effective.

Now of course Hempel does talk about history and explanation in history and it is reasonable to think that in doing so he makes claims about history and historians which could be erroneous even though what he says about explanation is general or in relation to science is not. And, it might be thought, it is in these claims that the connection between history and explanation which enables him and us to speak of historical explanation is to be found. Unfortunately, this is not the case. If Hempel had claimed as an empirical generalisation that all or almost all the explanations which we find in history books are roughly syllogistic in form and deductive or statistical he could be faulted by someone who pointed out that this is not so. But this is just what he does *not* claim. He says explicitly that the two schemata 'are not intended to reflect the manner in which working scientists [and this includes historians] actually formulate their explanatory accounts' (9: p. 85). Consequently, it cannot be an objection to his thesis that working scientists or historians do not actually proceed in the manner he suggests because he never claimed that they did. This rules out any straightforward appeal to the explanations in history books as a test of Hempel's thesis and leaves open to him two sorts of reply, both of which he does in fact employ. If someone claims to have found or to have seen an explanation which employs no general laws or probability statements, it is open to Hempel to argue that, though these may not appear in the explanation as it stands, they have to be supplied if the explanation is to be made complete. And this is just what he does argue in his discussion of F J Turner's explanation of the rapid advance of the Indian trader across the north American continent, which he describes as an 'explanation sketch'.

In the second place it is open to him to declare any counterexample from the history books not to be a case of explanation at all, precisely because it does not fit his model. On some occasions this reply has an air of cheating about it. If historians are prepared to call something an explanation why should we opt for Hempel's use of the term rather than theirs? But the cheating is more apparent than real. Hempel can simply deny that he has any obligation to accommodate all and every use of the term 'explanation' in his account, bearing in mind that common usage may be loose or inaccurate. In fact he says just this on one occasion, claiming that 'ordinary usage appears to provide no clear criterion for those arguments which are to be qualified as explanatory. This is not surprising for our every day concept of explanation is strongly influenced by preanalytic causal and teleological ideas; and these can hardly be expected to provide unequivocal guidance for a more formal and precise analysis of scientific explanation and prediction' (9: p. 10). He is after all offering a 'rational reconstruction' and it is a necessary feature of the attempt to offer a philosophical account of any concept that it should thus fail to cover any and every use of that concept. It follows from these two points that we cannot fix upon any instance from the history books which will do as a counterexample and to which Hempel cannot find a reply. It is to be observed, moreover, that the replies available to him are consistent with his thesis and do not involve any *ad hoc* emendations of it.

But the thought that Hempel cannot dodge every counterexample is hard to abandon and may lead to the suspicion that there is something wrong with any reconstruction of his model that enables it to do so. A parallel case can be used effectively to bring out what this might be.[4] Suppose Hempel were to have claimed that there is only one kind of large cat; it lives in social groups and the males have manes. It comes to our attention that some people have challenged Hempel's assertion with the claim that in India there lives a kind of cat which is solitary and has stripes. This 'Indian cat', for all we know, may be a fabulous monster, but it would surely be wrong to argue like this. There is no point in listening to Hempel's opponents in this debate because there are just two possibilities; either Hempel is right, in which case any cats there are in India will be lions and there is nothing interesting to be learned about *Indian* cats, or he is wrong, in which case since he said nothing about Indian cats only cats in general (Indian included) there is no point in examining claims about Indian cats. Besides, if he wants to, Hempel can wriggle out by claiming that all those stripey things are not really cats at all since they don't live in groups and the males have no manes.

If this is a strict parallel to my argument about Hempel and historical explanation then certainly something has gone wrong in it. But I do not think the parallel actually holds. There are three important points about it. First, the reason the argument about cats is so suspicious is that we are certain that our ability to identify cats when we see them is (a) pretty good and (b) not dependent on so few characteristics as those listed. Now my claim is that whether or not the cases of explanation the opponents of the covering law have produced really are explanations is, in many cases, genuinely under dispute, and in others that Hempel can *plausibly* call them explanation sketches. He thus has two ways of dealing with counterexamples neither of which is as obviously circular as the one way with cats. For the parallel to hold it would have to be the case that some tigers at least are not very obviously cats at all and of others that we can make out a case for thinking them to be lions in disguise. In the second place, where the parallel does hold it works to my advantage. It just is true that if Indian cats really exist their refutation of Hempel does not result from their solitary stripeyness but from their not being sociable and maned. Thus Hempel's generalisation certainly applies to cats in India but not to Indian cats so that to learn of the existence of tigers in India and that they really are cats is *not* to learn that there is a special species of cat called the 'Indian cat' and hence not to learn that Hempel is wrong because he didn't know about the 'Indian cat'. This parallels my earlier remark that if we can produce a convincing counterexample its coming from the pages of a history book will be quite incidental to its being effective. Thirdly, Hempel's imagined definition of 'large cat' is not a definitive one. Nobody could think that in it we have been given necessary and sufficient conditions of cathood. The parallel only has force because of the assumption of some background understanding of what are and what are not cats. In contrast, Hempel's model of explanation is meant to be definitive and can reasonably be thought to be so, even though it may prove erroneous in the long run. Thus, while it would be vacuously stipulative for Hempel to argue that tigers are not cats because they do not fit his description of lions, it is not equally foolish for him to claim the same of particular cases of explanation. It is for this reason that the deadlock between Hempel and his opponents cannot be broken by their counterexamples.

The parallel with lions and tigers, then, does not hold and I hope I have shown that my argument has more substance than might at first appear. In any case it is misleading to present my argument as allowing Hempel to dodge every counterexample. Indeed it is very important that he should *not* be able to do so since if all tests of this sort are inapplicable nothing entitles him to call his account an account of explanation. My point however is that not all kinds of counterexample will do. Counterexamples drawn from the realms of explanation in general will but counterexamples taken from the history books like those which Dray and Donagan produce will not.

The reason for this lies in two important differences between the two kinds of counterinstance. The examples from Salmon, Kyburg and Bromberger, if good, are cases which Hempel's models admit but which we should *not* regard as genuine cases of explanation, while the history book examples, conversely, are cases which Hempel's model does not admit as complete explanations and which it is said are perfectly good explanations as they stand. What is wanted if we are to succeed with the second sort is a case from the history books which on Hempel's account *is* an explanation but which our common knowledge or our intuitive grasp of the concept of explanation tells us is not one. If we were to produce such a case we should have done as much as Salmon has done, but we should have gone no distance towards establishing that there is something which Hempel's theory does not take account of which is historical explanation because, *ex hypothesi*, what we produced was not a case of explanation.

Secondly, and more importantly, as I pointed out earlier the first sort of counterexample relies for its effectiveness upon our having what may be called a pre-theoretical grasp of what is and what is not an explanation. The second sort must make some similar appeal. But in order to be more specific, this appeal must be to an unreflective understanding of what is and what is not an *historical* explanation. The trouble is that I do not think we have any linguistic intuitions in the second case of the sort we do have in the first. 'Historical explanation' is too sophisticated a concept for it to operate in this way.

I am entitled, then, to conclude, I think, that most modern discussions of historical explanation are wide of the mark. I do not mean to exonerate Hempel or the covering law theory, however. It is clear that Hempel does mean to say something about history. Indeed his two best known essays on the subject are entitled 'The Function of General Laws in History' and 'Explanation in Science and in History', but if I am right, whatever his intention, he has nothing to tell us about history or historical explanation at all. The source of this contradiction is not far to seek. Hempel is at his least lucid when he considers the relation between what he says about explanation and how the world goes, that is, in his conception of the relation between philosophy and its object. He does not think, as we have seen, that his business is merely to describe the practices of scientists and historians. He claims rather to be giving 'schemata . . . models . . . ideal types or theoretical idealisations . . . explications or rational reconstructions . . . or theoretical models . . . of certain modes of explanation' (9: p. 15). The variety of terminology alone is sufficient to generate confusion. But just as it is clear that he eschews mere description, so the expressions 'model', 'reconstruction' and 'explication' are enough to show that he does not wish to adopt a boldly prescriptive approach either. And if he did Salmon's examples demonstrate more than adequately that he could not avoid the charge of stipulative definition.

What then is the relation between the covering law theory and the actual business of explaining things? Whatever Hempel thinks, it must be, as I argued at the end of Chapter One, that his theory aims at, and its justification lies in, a reflective equilibrium between the demands of consistency, coherence and generality and our unreflective uses of the terms 'explain' and 'explanation'.

But if I am further right in thinking that there are no obvious or entrenched applications of the concept 'historical explanation' and that all uses of the expression will be to a degree reflective, how is the philosophical discussion of historical explanation to proceed? The answer, as I suggested in the first section, is that the concept needs to be introduced, its meaning and the range of its application explained and justified. This is what Hempel and his opponents do not do. They all suppose that what we mean by historical explanation is clear enough and that the business in hand is to say what it is like. This renders their appeal to the pages of history ineffectual.

Of course the same consideration renders ineffectual Hempel's appeals to history in support of his model, but this does not matter so much because he can always admit that the term 'historical' cannot be used to qualify explanation and that the connection between explanation and the study of history must be made in some other way. In point of fact Hempel himself seems reluctant to do this but others have done it in his defence. Thus May Brodbeck boldly asserts that 'There is no such thing as historical explanation, only the explanation of historical events' (4: p. 254) and others have rightly observed that 'this is entailed by the presuppositions of the covering law model' (2: p. 81).

Brodbeck's claim implies that we can forge a connection between history and explanation not in terms of the kind of explanation but in terms of the kind of thing to be explained. It is not the *explanans* but the *explanandum* which is peculiar to history. Leaving aside the question whether states of affairs might not admit of explanation as much as events, this seems promising. And yet it is far from clear that we can make much use of it. The suggestion appears to be that we can arrange the class of events into those that are historical and those that are not and that historians set themselves to explain the former exclusively. But if 'historical event' just means 'past event', as it often does, this classification is quite uninteresting. Future events cannot be explained, so they do not enter the calculation. Hempel thinks that only those events that have happened can be explained and if this is right, *all* explanations will be of historical, i.e. past events. Even if he is not right, the class of present events, those that have not yet ended, is so tiny that we will be no better informed about the peculiarities of history to be told that historians do not concern themselves with this class. Besides, it is not obviously true. The 'present' has no fixed temporal extension and I cannot see any reason for thinking that an historian could not set out to explain the advent of the Second World War in, say, 1942.

On an alternative interpretation the expression 'historical event' means any particular or unique or nameable event. The events scientists explain, it might be said, are instances of types of events, and the scientist has no interest in the particularity of the event, or if you like, the event in itself. It is this which marks him off from the historian, who is interested in an event in its particularity. Brodbeck's remark thus becomes the suggestion that the explanation of particular events is no different in form from the explanation of instances of types of events. This way of characterising the difference between the scientist and the historian is close to Popper's view in *The Open Society and its Enemies*. Here he declares that in

the so-called theoretical or generalizing sciences (such as physics, biology, sociology, etc.) we are predominantly interested in universal laws or hypo-

theses. . . . Our interest in the specific events, for example in experiments
which are described by the initial conditions and prognoses, is somewhat
limited; we are interested in them mainly as means to certain ends, means by
which we can test the universal laws. . . . Now the sciences which have [an]
interest in specific events and their explanation may, in contradistinction to the
generalizing sciences, be called the historical sciences (35: pp. 447–448).

It is certain that there is something right about this. Especially
important is the fact that the contrast here is not between history and
science but between the theoretical and the historical, and I shall say
more about this at a later stage. Nonetheless, in the context of this
examination of Hempel and the covering law model Popper's claim is
importantly wrong. In the first place the distinction it makes between the
sciences is a matter of cast of mind, the interests people happen to have.
Perhaps this is not wholly wrong but on the face of it at least it is
historians and physicists, not history and physics, which are capable of
having and taking interests. Consequently, if we mean to distinguish
between the disciplines rather than the practitioners, as Popper plainly
means to do, there must be more to be said. Otherwise his remarks
amount to a bit of amateur psychology. In the second place, despite the
fact that Popper's view has a great deal in common with Hempel's and
Brodbeck's, he is here claiming the opposite of the view they espouse. On
Popper's account, properly speaking, only particular events can be
explained, so that all explanations will be of historical events, whether or
not we are interested in their particularity. Hempel, on the other
hand, thinks that wholly particularised, nameable events 'cannot be
explained by covering laws or in any other way. Indeed it is unclear what
could be meant by explaining such an event' (10: p. 150).

The point I want to make here is that whoever is right about this we do
not have a useful classification of events. If Popper is right, to speak of
the explanation of historical events will be to speak of all those events
which can be explained. If Hempel is right, to speak of the explanation
of historical events in this sense will be nonsense.

Perhaps none of this has much to do with Brodbeck. She means to distinguish, as indeed Hempel does, I think, between the events of human
and social life and those of the natural world. Thus, the cracking of my
car radiator last winter, a well-known example of Hempel's, is, for
Brodbeck, less than 'properly historical'. Now the distinction between
historical and natural events is a very familiar one and plays an important part in the philosophy of explanation, yet it is rarely examined. I
want to argue that the distinction between actions and events can be as
radical or fundamental as you like and still make no difference to the
nature of historical explanation. But I shall reserve my discussion of the

distinction until the next chapter and end this one by taking note of the point we have reached.

I have argued that the famous covering law theory of explanation does not and cannot generate any account of what it means to call an explanation historical. Indeed, it gives us no reason to employ such a concept, one of which we have, I assert, no intuitive grasp. The course of the argument has led us to think that the only way in which the covering law model of explanation can be made to say anything about history lies in the suggestion that the *explananda* of historical inquiry are distinctive or peculiar. This is, surprisingly, one of the principal doctrines of Hempel's opponents and it is in connection with their arguments that I want to examine it.

4

Rational explanation, history and nature

While it is true that debates about historical explanation have most often begun with a discussion of Hempel's theory, his critics have not contented themselves with proving him to be wrong but have offered positive replacements for what they take to be his erroneous doctrine. In addition philosophers in the tradition rightly or wrongly called Idealist, notably Collingwood and Oakeshott, elaborated their conceptions of history before Hempel's work appeared.[5] It is to the examination of these alternatives that I now turn. As in the last section I shall not be interested in whether the theories are sound so much as whether they give us any account of what it means to call an explanation historical. And I shall argue that they do not.

It would be difficult to examine all the alternatives to Hempel within reasonable compass and I shall not try to do so. But the point I want to make will be borne out well enough if I can show what is going wrong in some of the better known alternatives. Amongst these the book by W H Dray from which I have been quoting is one of the most powerful critiques of the covering law model, and indeed one of the best books on the subject. It has provoked almost as much discussion as the theory it attacks for in the positive part of the book Dray tries to rehabilitate one of the traditional doctrines of idealist philosophers of history. For this reason its examination will be the examination of a more general alternative view to Hempel's. Dray argues for the view that 'the objects of historical study are fundamentally different from those, for example, of the natural sciences, because they are the actions of beings like ourselves; and that even if (for the sake of the argument) we allow that natural events may be explained by subsuming them under empirical laws, it would still be true that this procedure is inappropriate in history' (23:

p. 118). Two observations are in order here. The first is that my arguments of the last section have not been set against straw men. Dray makes it plain in this passage that in his view Hempel could be right about science and still wrong about history and this, I have argued, is impossible. Secondly, the distinction between 'natural' and 'historical' comes to the fore here and what is more, some account of the distinction is presupposed, namely, that it coincides pretty well with the distinction between actions and events. This presupposition is important because the belief that the difference between explanation in science and explanation in history, if any, is the same as the difference between the explanation of natural events and the explanation of actions is to be found in a great deal that has been written in the philosophy of history. But I shall argue that, even if the latter distinction is well drawn, this tells us nothing about explanation in history and in science.

If we suppose that Dray is right to think that the explanation of human actions must differ radically from the explanation of natural events and even that the explanation of actions takes the form he says it does, namely, 'a display of the *rationale* of what was done' (ibid. p. 124), then he has given us an account of the explanation of actions and of what it is for something to be a rational explanation. But he has not told us what it is about these rational explanations that enables or entitles us to call them historical. He has given us no reason to think that the explanation of action in history is to be marked off in any interesting way from the explanation of action in everyday life. Indeed, he admits as much when he adds to his account of historical explanation the remark that 'if the agent is to understand his *own* actions, i.e. after the event, he may have to do so by constructing a calculation in exactly the same way [as the historian does]' (ibid. p. 123). But if there is no difference between the explanation of the objects of historical study and the explanation of our own actions, Dray's account, even if it is correct in every detail, has no more to tell us about *historical* explanation than Hempel's did.

It is hard to avoid the feeling that this objection is a matter of quibbling about words. If Dray is right and actions cannot be explained in the way that natural events are and if, as is obviously the case, historians are in large part, perhaps the largest part, interested in explaining the actions of those they study, hasn't Dray told us something important about history, whatever one wishes to call the type of explanation he describes? The only point of philosophical interest is whether he is right about the explanation of action or not. But however strongly we feel inclined to argue in this way the fact is that we have not been given any foundation for the use of a term, 'historical explanation', which is nonetheless widely used. Now I do not want to deny that Dray has something important to say, right or wrong, about explanation and *a fortiori* about the explanation of action by historians. But if this is all, the relation of his remarks to history is quite incidental. In exactly the same sense he has something to say about the explanation of actions by sports commentators (which as a matter of fact he does (p. 158)), but not enough to justify him or us in talking about 'sporting explanations' and thinking that we have picked out a type of explanation by our talk. So why should it be thought that the position is any better with regard to historical explanation? If it is said that the chief interest in Dray's work lies in his account of the explanation of actions, we have then the choice of abandoning all reference to historical explanation, a course I am not unwilling to adopt, or of explaining wherein the connection between rational and historical explanation lies; and in a way that will enable us to pick out of the total class of explanations (or explanations of actions) those that are to be called historical.

I shall offer my own view on the first alternative later on, but I want to notice here that Dray could hardly accept it. In the first place he criticises Gardiner and Popper for just the reason that I have criticised him here, arguing against Gardiner's criterion of historical explanation that it would 'admit as specifically historical *all* the explanations given in daily life which are framed in ordinary language' (p. 83) and against Popper's criterion that though 'it has the merit of distinguishing between historical and non-historical within the class marked off by Gardiner as non-technical. Yet his criterion, like Gardiner's, is too broad, for it cuts across the class of technical (i.e. scientific) explanations as well' (p. 8). In the second place Dray makes his own concern quite clear. It is with 'the logic of history, interpreting "logic" in the broad sense made familiar by contemporary analytic philosophers. It is not epistemology or psychology' (ibid. p. 21).

It seems then that the first course is not open to him. Someone might suppose, however, that he could at least replace the expression 'historical explanation' by the expression 'explanation in history' and make the connection which the second course requires in this way. In point of fact I do not think that Dray can do so very easily both because it ill accords with his criticism of Gardiner and because of some of the things he says, but let us ignore this and ask simply in what way this would make the required connection, how, that is to say, it would relate what Dray says about the explanation of action specifically or peculiarly to history. I argued in the last section that appeals to the pages of history are, for quite general reasons, ineffective against Hempel. For similar reasons they appear to be ineffective in support of Dray. One cannot prove by examples, even examples as illuminating as Dray's, and if the phrase 'explanation in history' means 'the explanations historians give' it seems that what is called for is something philosophers, Dray no less than others, do not normally regard themselves as having to engage in, i.e. an exhaustive survey of the history books designed to discover whether as a matter of empirical fact the explanation of actions in terms of their rationale does indeed predominate over explanations of other types. I say 'it seems' because of course this procedure is not altogether straightforward. We have first to decide which books to survey and what weight we are going to give to the relevant items we find there and this is not something we can do without some prior understanding of what history is and what explanation is. Consequently the results of our survey are unlikely to settle much. Even if these difficulties were avoidable, a positive result would still fail to establish any special relation between rational explanation and explanation in history because it would give us no reason to think that positive results would not be obtained in surveys of other classes of books.

In any case, Dray does not proceed in this way. He contents himself with observing (a) that rational explanation is characteristic of history and (b) that historians seem to have an expressed preference for explanations of this sort. The weakness of the second point he acknowledges himself, declaring that he does not mean that 'no trace of [the covering law model] will be found at all in the explanations historians normally give' (ibid. p. 19) and that 'if [for example] a psychological theory were necessary and available to explain Monck's "cryptic" behaviour, [i.e. a non-rational explanation] it would be the historian's business to use it' (ibid. p. 139). With regard to the first point the position is no different from that of the empirical survey. 'Characteristic', it is true, does not mean 'numerically preponderant' but we have still to decide which body of literature we are trying to characterise. Dray and his opponents are not agreed about this. White and Hempel both think that there is no significant difference between history and sociology for the purposes of analysing explanation while Dray regards them as very importantly different. He is likely, therefore, to be unmoved by some of the examples they urge against his characterisation, for instance, the case of Parkinson's law, which Hempel discusses at some length. He, on the other hand, thinks that history is 'logically continuous' with literature while they are likely to hold that explanation in literature does not bear upon the question at all, given their interest in the unity of the empirical sciences amongst which literature is clearly not to be numbered. Even if these differences are settled it remains the case that Dray must have some reason to exclude explanation in natural history before he can characterise explanation in history as the rational explanation of action. And this reason must be quite independent of what he says about explanation in history and the explanation of action, otherwise his thesis becomes the trivially true claim that the explanation of human actions in history characteristically employs the mode of explanation appropriate to human actions. But we do not find any such reason in Dray's book because in reality his chief concern is with action and he takes the connection with history to be perfectly obvious. The question of natural history is not discussed at all.

It is right to think, of course, that this does not matter as long as some such reason can be supplied. If we could show that the concept of an historical event excludes natural events and thus that the expression 'natural history' *is* something of a self-contradiction, we would thereby establish a special relationship between rational explanation as Dray describes it and the study of history. I shall turn to this possibility in a moment. But for Dray's account as it stands the end result is the same as it is for the covering law theory, namely, that everything turns upon the unrecognised need to establish some clear distinction between natural and historical events. This is no coincidence. Like Hempel, Dray aims to say something about history and historians and like him, in the conclusions he reaches, this is just what he fails to do. The source of the failure is the same in both cases. Dray is no more clear about the relation between philosophical analysis and the practice of historians. On the one hand he praises Gardiner for his 'desire to illuminate what the historian actually does' and on the other hand he faults him for taking ' "historical explanation" to be equivalent to "explanation found in history books" ' on the grounds that this cannot meet the legitimate philosophical demand for generality since, on this definition, 'it is unlikely that we shall find any *logical* features according to which all historical explanations can be grouped together as historical' because 'the explanations found in history books are a logically miscellaneous lot' (ibid. p. 85). As criticisms of Gardiner these may be just. My point is that Dray has not isolated any 'logical feature' according to which all historical explanations may be grouped together as historical either. At best what he has done is to show what logical features explanations of action have in common such that they may all be described as rational explanations. But the connection between historical explanation and the explanation of action has not been established.

This is an appropriate point at which to turn to Collingwood because his views are similar to Dray's and he explicitly tries to make this connection. We commonly think, as Dray evidently does, that properly speaking history is the history of human affairs, and the activity and opinions of those we know to be historians tend to confirm us in this belief. But Collingwood recognises that once we raise doubts about this belief 'it is not enough to consider the characteristics of history as it actually exists, for the question at issue is whether, as it actually exists, it covers the whole field which properly belongs to it' (18: p. 213). In other words, we may be inclined to think that the connection between history and human action, and hence the connection between historical explanation and the explanation of action, is a natural and obvious one, but once we observe the fact that the natural world appears to have a history as well, we must ask whether the human world is the only possible object of historical investigation, and more importantly, whether there is any special relationship between historical method and the study of human action at all.

According to Collingwood, however, our intuitive judgements are correct in fact. In an important sense nature does not admit of historical understanding. His argument runs as follows. The historian distinguishes between two aspects of any event, its 'inside' and its 'outside'. The outside of an event is 'everything belonging to it which can be described in terms of bodies and their movements'. The inside is that which can only be described in terms of thought. Now 'in the case of nature this distinction between the outside and the inside of an event does not arise. The events of nature are mere events. . . . It is true that the scientist, like the historian, has to go beyond the mere discovery of events; but the direction in which he moves is very different. . . . He goes beyond the event, but only to observe its relation to others and to bring it under a general law or formula'. Consequently, 'The processes of nature can therefore be properly described as sequences of mere events, but those of history cannot. They are not processes of mere events but processes of actions which have an inner side, consisting of processes of thought. All history is the history of thought' (ibid: pp. 213–215).

Plainly, Collingwood thinks that he is giving us reason to employ a sharp distinction between history and nature here, but he is doing nothing of the sort. The assertion with which he begins, that the historian distinguishes between two aspects of any event, one of which is its thought side, begs the question since it is just another way of saying that the historian is exclusively concerned with action. Not surprisingly it follows that the historian has no interest in nature. But the argument is no argument at all. It simply asserts what it is supposed to show.

It is unusual to find Collingwood producing such a poor argument. We ought to remember, of course, that his book was put together after his death[6] and in fact I do not think that much of what he says about history need depend upon this argument. For unlike all the other writers I have been considering Collingwood never uses the expression 'historical explanation'. His concern is with historical understanding and there is a sense in which the only past events an historian can hope to *understand* are human actions, though these are not the only past events he can hope to explain. When the natural historian, Darwin for instance, sets himself to discover the course of natural history, he wishes not only to record what happened but to discover the processes at work in its coming about. Thus, though he may explain the appearance of the Galapagos Islands, it is the process of volcanic eruption which admits of being understood. It is quite in order to speak of explaining the existence of the islands, odd to speak of understanding their existence. By way of contrast, it seems right to speak of understanding the actions of Louis XIV with respect to William of Orange, say, whether or not we can say or hope to say what generalisable processes are at work here. This is not an argument so much as a suggestion that there may be an important distinction to make between understanding the events of human and those of natural history which captures everything that is important to Collingwood, but if there is, it is not one which lends any support to those interested in explanation.

I have argued that Hempel, Brodbeck and Dray all imply that there is some special and obvious connection between history and human affairs such that to say something about the explanation of human action, that it is the same as or different from the explanation of other phenomena, is to have said something about historical explanation without making explicit any reason for thinking that this is the case. And Collingwood, who does argue this point explicitly, gives us no reason to draw any distinction relevant to the explanation of events, whatever the relation of his argument to his own thesis. Of course, what these writers say does not exhaust all the possibilities of argument. Someone might claim, for instance, that though it makes sense to speak of natural or medical history, we have a sufficiently clear grasp of the character of history to be able to declare the study of these peripheral compared to the centrality of political or economic history. As evidence of this we might note how misleading it would be for a biologist or geologist to call himself an historian. But this argument will not work either. Biology and geology are not wholly, perhaps not even chiefly, concerned with natural history, it is true, but it does not follow that there would be anything misleading about calling an historian someone who *was* concerned solely with geological history. If it is said that he would have to qualify his title with the word 'natural' in order to avoid misleading people, this does not establish much. In exactly the same way someone interested in the history of art must call himself an *art* historian, for art history is peripheral in just the way that natural history is here said to be, that is, it does not concern most historians most of the time. In any case, if the claim is that the proper title for a geologist, or better, geomorphologist, is 'scientist', this presupposes just the contrast between history and science that is at issue. Why shouldn't we say that this branch of geology is an historical science?

The point, however, is not to argue about titles but to show that several familiar lines of argument go no way towards establishing the sort of distinction between history and the natural world that is so often taken for granted and upon which the relevance of Dray's argument and the arguments of the idealists depend. One could, no doubt, go on examining possible distinctions and the arguments adduced to support them indefinitely but I do not propose to do so. Instead I want to terminate the discussion of this point with the observation that it seems both evident and reasonable to hold that nature has a history and that we can explain why its past was as it was. If this is so, any account of historical explanation must cover these explanations too. The thought that there are other and perhaps better arguments which have not been considered need not trouble us because, by the end of the essay, I hope to have shown that there is a clear, obvious and intelligible criterion of historical explanation which we can adopt without having to assert or deny any distinction which may be made between the human and the natural worlds.

This section has been concerned largely with Dray and his alternative to the covering law model. I have argued that, whatever its merits as an account of the explanation of human action, Dray's thesis is seriously deficient as an account of historical explanation. This deficiency has been noticed elsewhere, in the essay by Terence Ball from which I quoted earlier. Ball recognises the need to set out just what it is about historical explanations that makes them historical, regardless of the kind of event that is explained. He offers two senses in which an explanation might be said to be historical. The second of these he describes as 'a rather queer species of historical explanation' and certainly it does not bear upon the argument here directly. The first sense he offers as a remedy to the deficiency I have detected in Dray, and it is this sense that is of most interest in the present context.

According to Ball the structure of explanation is the same for Dray as it is for Hempel,[7] i.e. deductive. The difference is that whereas the covering law model, as its name implies, invokes a universal law as the major premise, in Dray it is a principle of action which serves in this place. Thus instead of

$$\frac{C_1, C_2, \ldots C_k}{L_1, L_2, \ldots L_k}$$
$$\therefore E$$

we have

> A was in C
> A believes X the thing to do in C-type circumstances.
> _____
> $\therefore A$ does X

Once this is clear we can see that Dray's criticism of the covering law theory is not radically different from other criticisms less concerned with the explanation of action and 'in fact, Dray's principle of action, Scriven's normic statements and Rescher's, Joynt's and Helmer's quasi-laws are more similar than dissimilar. For all are statements which are neither universal, (merely) statistical, nor summative of particular instances; and all belong, moreover, to the class of "E-type" statements, in as much as they may be construed as rules or principles which historical agents use to guide and justify their conduct, and (*pace* Kant) which they have adopted as maxims of behaviour' (2: p. 183). Now the point about these quasi-laws is that they can be 'historically situated and subject to decay, revision and revocation' whereas the universal laws of the covering law theory cannot be. It is this fact which enables us to speak of specifically historical explanation. 'An historical explanation is one in which at least one "law" statement in the *explanans* is subject to historical placement or temporal location. Outside these historical limits this "law" is false or unintelligible. . . . For example, the convention of primogeniture may figure in the explanation of some acts of emigration at one time (e.g. the colonial period of American history) but would not figure in any and all emigrations and at any and every time (e.g. today). Second sons still emigrate from Europe to America, to be sure, but no longer for precisely the same reasons for which second sons emigrated two hundred years ago' (2: p. 184).

Ball describes his suggestion as a 'simple emendation' of Dray's account and this is its charm. Dray holds that in the explanation of action any general statement we employ 'would express a judgement of the form: "When in a situation of type $C_1 \ldots C_n$ the thing to do is X"' (23 p. 132). Ball adds 'by a class of agents in some historically determinate time and place' (2: p. 185). The importance of this addition is considerable in the context of my argument. I have claimed that if Hempel is right we have no reason to call any explanation an historical one and that appeals to what historians do or to a distinction between historical and other events are of no assistance. Equally, if Dray is right, though we may have reason to call some explanations rational, we still have no clear idea of what it means to describe an explanation as historical. Ball's criterion, however, enables us to pick out of the class of explanations, or the class of rational explanations, a subset which we have reason to call historical. Thus Ball's argument is the only one encountered so far which is on the right lines and its examination will further show this to be the case. But at the same time it will reveal the inadequacy of his definition. First, however, we can in fact strengthen his argument, for it has two unnecessary weaknesses.

The first of these concerns the examples he uses, for these are not altogether satisfactory. His express concern is with the explanation of action by reference to rules which license, prescribe or proscribe certain sorts of action, yet it is doubtful if the examples he gives us are actually of this kind. Consider the case of primogeniture and the emigration of second sons. I do not suppose that Ball wishes to assert in the absence of any evidence that the convention of primogeniture does not figure in the explanation of *any* present day emigration from Europe to America. The point, I take it, is rather that what was a common reason once is common no longer. If this is the point then what is explained is the generality of a particular phenomenon at one historical period by reference to the historically bounded *fact* that many people were guided by this convention. It is not an historically bounded *rule* that is employed in the explanation. Unless this is a case of 'figuring in'. But then 'figure in' is too vague and does not tell us clearly enough how the principle is related to the explanation. I have a similar sort of objection to Ball's second example. To explain 'why no Samurai presently hold high political office in Japan' by telling someone 'that they are barred from political office by the terms of the post-war Japanese constitution' looks to me like the explanation of a social statistic, not the explanation of an action in history. I am not sure how far Ball would consider my doubts about his examples to be real difficulties but in any case their inadequacy, if that is what it is, does not matter very much. It is clear what he has in mind and it is not hard to find better examples. Consider, for instance, the puzzling fact that, despite his knowledge of and belief in Philip II's tyrannical misrule of the Netherlands, in his published proclamation William the Silent chose to justify his rebellion not by reference to Philip's mistreatment of his subjects but by a list of the personal injuries and slights which he, William, had received at Philip's hands. The action is to be explained and the puzzle resolved once we understand the conceptions and conventions of feudalism, according to which the relationship between vassal and overlord, being a moral rather than a political one, is broken by personal injury, not by political ineptitude. Or again we may be puzzled by the curious reaction of Peter Abelard to the news that the pupil he had seduced, Heloise, was pregnant, for, though a clerk in Holy Orders, he offers to legitimise her position by marriage while insisting that the marriage be kept secret. More puzzling still, perhaps, is her refusal to accept, when it is evident that she was passionately devoted to him. The explanation is to be found in the details of canon law and the ideals of monastic life, in other words in laws and customs which are no longer part of our social life. In both these cases, then, rules, once widely understood but which have passed out of currency, must be employed in the explanation of action.

The second point at which Ball's claim could be strengthened relates to the explanation of natural events. When he addresses a possible objection to his thesis, the objection that 'even the best laws of physics are only approximately valid, holding true only within certain limitations or boundary conditions', he appears to contrast history and physics in much the way that those who have wanted to draw a sharp distinction between history and nature have done, but if he does, this is an unnecessary limitation upon his criterion. Morton White has argued, convincingly to my mind, that law-like generalisations about individuals can be employed in the explanation and prediction of events in exactly the way universal laws can. He offers this example from Dickens:

> 'Newman, I shouldn't be surprised if my brother were dead.'
> 'I don't think you would' said Newman quietly.
> 'Why not, sir?' demanded Mr Nickleby.
> 'You never are surprised' replied Newman, 'that's all' (39: p. 50).

Likewise, the generalisation that Hitler hated all those he thought were Jews enables us to explain his attitude towards a certain person by reference to the fact that he thought he was a Jew. The general point is that 'regularism . . . does not require its advocates to hold that the general laws offered in support of singular explanatory statements "apply to all times and places"'. Now perhaps it is true, as Ball says, that the laws physics employs apply to all times and places, but this need not be the case for the explanation of all natural events. For instance, a geomorphologist might explain the existence and character of a geographical feature by appeal to some general property of the ice sheet which once covered a particular area. In this case his explanation employs a temporally bounded generalisation and is historical as Ball defines it. We do not, then, have reason to restrict historical explanation to human actions and affairs.

Having, as I think, strengthened Ball's account of historical explanation in these two respects, we can now proceed to its examination. Consider the following example. Jones is on his way to the payroll office. The explanation is to be found in the facts that this is Friday, it is part of Jones's job to collect the wages for his section, and the wages are made up on Friday. In this explanation we make appeal to a principle of action governing the behaviour of anyone in Jones's position and to a set of conditions. The principle has a temporal location, namely the present, so the explanation is an historical one on Ball's definition. But having explained a present action by reference to conditions obtaining in the present and a principle of action at present in operation, what reason could we have to call our explanation an historical one? I have thrown considerable doubt upon the efficacy of counterexamples and it may be thought that it ill becomes me to appeal to one now. But the example has some force. In the first place, given that there is no reference to the past in it anywhere, we at least have reason *not* to describe it as historical, and the only reason we have to do so is the rather arbitrary assertion by Ball that because it has a temporally located rule in it we should. In the second place, Ball must allow some weight to the counterinstance since, as I have done, he criticises Dray and other opponents of the covering law model for making 'no distinction between explanations in history and those offered and accepted in everyday life, in the law, and in other presumably non-historical activities' (2: p. 182).

It might be said that my example is not an historical explanation on Ball's definition because the principle of action it employs, since it is in operation at present and indefinitely into the future, is not historically bounded. But this reply affords only momentary relief. In his example of the Samurai and Japanese government Ball allows that a principle of action can be historically bounded when it seems 'a safe bet that . . . it will not figure as a principle of (Japanese political) action very much longer' (ibid: p. 185). If anticipation of the future course of events will do to lend an explanatory principle historical boundaries, we can easily import into my example the fact that it has been decided, from next week on say, to change the day upon which the wages are made up. In this case the principle invoked to explain Jones's action does have precise historical boundaries, but it is still the explanation of a present event in terms of conditions and principles which hold at present; we still have no reason to call it historical.

If anyone has residual doubts about the matter, the inadequacy of Ball's definition can be set out even more plainly. Let us suppose that Jones makes some plan in anticipation of the fact that for the next three weeks he will go to the payroll office on Thursday, the rule having been changed accordingly. Here a temporally located principle figures in the explanation of Jones's planning activities. The trouble is that its temporal location, though very precise, is in the future and it would be very odd to call our explanation of his plan historical *for this reason*. At the very least we have good reason *not* to call it this.

Ball calls anything an historical explanation if 'one "law" (or better, perhaps, quasi-law) in the *explanans* is tensed or temporally located', but clearly this is not enough. We need the past tense, or temporal location in the past. If we make this alteration we do indeed have a class of explanations which we have reason to call historical explanations. Thus we can say that the explanation of William the Silent's proclamation is historical for it refers us to a rule of conduct obtaining in the past, a tensed sentence, as Ball has it, but importantly in the past tense. This amendment is so small that we might be inclined to think that his definition remains substantially correct. But this is not so. It is the amendment that is doing all the work and not the substance of the definition at all. This is evident once we observe that the 'law' or 'quasi-law' is, by everyone's admission, only one part of the explanans. The other part, the statement of initial conditions, may also be in the past tense, and if it is, we have as much reason to call the explanation historical as we do if the quasi-law is in the past tense. Consider the explanation of Henry VIII's ascent to the throne. Henry became heir, even though he was not the first born son, because his elder brother Arthur died of a fever brought on by playing tennis. The rule of succession employed in this explanation is, as far as I know, still that in operation, but we have reason to call the explanation an historical one because it refers us to the events which preceded his accession. In short, it explains the event in terms of its history. And in fact, as I shall try to show in the remainder of this essay, this characterisation of historical explanation is sufficient. We need presuppose nothing about the temporal boundaries of any law or quasi-law involved, or even that it has temporal boundaries at all.

5

A definition and some objections

I ended the last chapter with the claim that to give an historical explanation of some event or state of affairs is to give its history. For any explanation which fulfils this definition it is obvious why we should and would call it an historical one. Let me stress this point. My claim is that if the explanation of a particular fact refers us to its history, i.e. its past, it is evident that we have reason to call it an historical explanation and it is clear what we mean by this. We have, then, a minimal definition or basic proposition of the kind I described in Chapter 1, that is, a clear, obvious and intelligible criterion of what is to count as an historical explanation. I claim that this criterion is clear, intelligible and obvious. But these very features may make it worthless, or, what amounts to the same thing, wholly devoid of philosophical interest. In this chapter I propose to consider a number of objections to it which, in one way or another, have this as their conclusion. In fact I shall find them all unconvincing, but the conclusion to which they point has some truth in it. Subsequent argument will show, I think, that properly understood historical explanation is not a topic which presents any aspects of great philosophical interest and that the study of history may not involve many of the philosophical problems that some writers claim to have found in it. But some clarity may yet be brought to the subject and, as I hope to show, considerable advantages will be found to flow from this.

It may be useful to adumbrate the objections I am about to examine. They are four. It might be held that:

(1) The definition encompasses explanations we should not want to call historical.

(2) *All* explanations are historical on this definition. It therefore fails to mark any distinction.

(3) The definition can be shown to be trivial and empty.
(4) The definition is without interest since it tells us nothing at all about the study of history.

1. The account of historical explanation I have proposed is scarcely novel. Indeed according to Morton White writing in 1942, it has been very widely held to be substantially correct. He says this in the essay 'Historical Explanation', one theme of which I have already discussed, and it is part of the point of that essay to refute the claim that 'an historical explanation explains facts prevailing at one time by reference to facts prevailing at an earlier time' (16: p. 212). This is a view indistinguishable from the definition I have offered and his objection to it is as follows:

> . . . there are explanations which would be called physical, others which would be called chemical and others which would be called biological, all of which must be called historical on the view. For instance, if one explains the relative positions of the sun, the moon and the earth, by reference to their relative positions one year ago, one is giving an *historical* explanation on the view under consideration. Obviously the statement of their positions one year ago expresses a fact earlier than the one which expresses their present positions. Furthermore, the laws of mechanics which figure in the explanation connect facts prevailing at different times. But we do not want our analysis to result in the statement that one explanation is both mechanical and historical. One of the conditions we impose on our analysis is that it permits us to deny this possibility. Put in other words, we are assuming that the phrase 'historical explanation' is so used that we cannot say of an explanation, without impropriety, that it is both physical and historical. It is not my intention to deny that one could use the phrase 'historical explanation' so that historical explanations (in this arbitrary sense) would turn up in all the sciences. . . . But if we are interested in analysing what is actually meant by the phrase 'historical explanation' we should do well to assign another name to the class of explanations that explain present facts in terms of past facts (ibid: p. 215–216).

This argument is endorsed by Dray. He says, of Popper's version of the same criterion, that

> it would, for instance, classify as historical the explanations of a chemistry demonstrator of the changed colour of a piece of litmus paper after being dipped in an acid solution. The statement 'it was dipped in that acid solution' sets out a 'singular initial condition' but it would hardly be regarded as giving anything which we should normally call an historical explanation. For the real work of the explanation is done by a chemical theory which the demonstrator knows how to apply to the case. And although White's analysis was in other ways unsatisfactory, he was surely right to insist that no criterion which allows an overlap of, say, 'historical' and 'chemical' explanations could be acceptable (23: pp. 83–84).

This argument is repeated time and again[8] in the literature and yet it constitutes a classic instance of begging the question. Like Collingwood's it assumes what it is supposed to establish. It is only after we have been told what is peculiar to historical explanation that we can say whether the epithets 'historical' and 'chemical' or 'physical' are incompatible. We cannot *show* that they are by declaring that they are. Moreover, the appeal which both White and Dray make to ordinary usage is quite ineffectual. They imply that outside of philosophy we have a clear idea of what we should normally say. But I deny that this is so, since, outside of philosophy, I do not think that the expression 'historical explanation' is widely used at all. Which of us is right does not matter, however. Let us suppose that widely and commonly the expression 'historical explanation' is reserved for explanations of human actions and social affairs. Once we raise the question whether there is good reason to restrict it in this way Collingwood's point, in a slightly amended version, comes into play: 'it is not enough to consider the characteristics history is normally thought to have, for the question at issue is whether, as it is normally conceived, it covers the whole field which properly belongs to it'. In short, the appeal to normal usage, even if there is a normal usage, effects nothing.

It might be said that this reply does not properly address White's account of historical explanation. He allows that the expression can be used in the way laid down by my definition and is quite open about making it one of the conditions of his analysis that the epithets 'physical' and 'historical', when used to qualify explanation, should be mutually exclusive. Why should he not remain free to do this? Indeed he is free to do so, but he also wants to claim that to use the expression in accordance with my definition would be arbitrary whereas, if I am right, it is his restrictive condition that is arbitrary. It might also be thought that I have overlooked Dray's remark that in the litmus paper example the real work of the explanation is being done by a chemical theory. But in fact this is just an assertion on his part. Michael Scriven has made the point that we can often explain facts, like the inkstain on my carpet, by referring to what happened (I knocked the bottle over with my elbow) when we are quite ignorant of the physical and chemical laws which are undoubtedly involved. Similarly, though perhaps the chemistry demonstrator does have the knowledge needed to explain the action of acid on litmus paper, in explaining how the paper got to be red he only has to refer to what happened to it and the low level knowledge that acid has this effect. What is true, of course, is that the point of his demonstration is likely to concern acid and litmus paper and he will have little or no interest in *this* piece of paper, but this does not affect the point I am making here.

In the light of my discussion of the distinction between history and nature in the last section I hope enough has been said to show that the common assumption which appears here in the form of the claim that the expressions 'physical explanation' and 'historical explanation' are necessarily incompatible is unwarranted. We may therefore dismiss the first objection on the list.

2. We have seen that common linguistic usage, even if it were uniform and contrary to my criterion (which it is not), would not suffice to overturn it. Let us consider now the suggestion that the definition I advanced fails because it renders *all* explanations in this sense historical and thus prevents us from making any discriminations whatever. The ground of this objection is not hard to see. Just those explanations which are offered by Hempel as examples from the natural sciences, the cracking of a car radiator during a cold, frosty night, the appearance of soap bubbles from under the rim of a tumbler that has just been washed, the drop in the level of mercury in a thermometer immersed in hot water, are all historical on the definition since each of them refers to a preceding event. The point may be made in a quite general way. All events (save possibly the Big Bang) take place in time and space and must therefore be preceded by some other event. Consequently the explanation of any event will refer to a preceding event. This, however, is what all writers on the subject admit. All accounts of explanation allow some place to initial conditions and disputes have arisen only over the nature of the link that is to be made between initial conditions and *explanandum* event. To define historical explanation in the manner proposed is certainly to transcend this dispute but only because it makes central that feature of explanation upon which all are agreed. The effect of this, however, is to make *all* explanations historical and thus to produce a classification which prevents any attempt at differentiation.

The fault with this objection is that the implication it draws from the definition just does not follow. At most what is true is that, if I am right, every event must have an historical explanation. It does not follow that events can only have historical explanations and indeed there are several other kinds of explanation to which we might point. But even if it did follow, this does not make all explanations historical for there is no reason to think that events are the only things we wish to or can explain. Consider Hempel's examples of scientific explanation again. Hempel offers these as simple cases of the sort of explanation scientists employ and aim to provide. But are they? We should note first of all a systematic ambiguity in all of them. For instance in 'Studies in the Logic of Explanation' (with Paul Oppenheim) he explores the following case:

A mercury thermometer is rapidly immersed in hot water; there occurs a temporary drop in the mercury column, which is then followed by a swift rise. How is this phenomenon to be explained? (11: p. 9)

What *exactly* is the phenomenon to be explained? Is it the behaviour of this thermometer or is it the observed regularity in the behaviour of thermometers? Hempel and Oppenheim's way of expressing it is compatible with two quite distinct phenomena: (i) a mercury thermometer was rapidly immersed in water; its column of mercury dropped temporarily and then rose swiftly; (ii) whenever a mercury thermometer is rapidly immersed in hot water, the mercury column falls temporarily and then rises swiftly. The difference between the two is crucial. In the first case the phenomenon to be explained is a dateable event—the sudden drop and subsequent rise in the column of mercury. It thus admits of an historical explanation on my definition, i.e. an explanation in terms of what exactly happened to the thermometer, including the fact that it was immersed in hot water. In the second case, it is a regularity which is to be explained and a regularity is *not* an event, being introduced by the term 'whenever' rather than the term 'when'. In other words regularities are atemporal. One important consequence of this observation is that Hempel's two schemata *cannot* be right, since each makes reference to initial conditions, and where what we have to deal with are regularities, there are no initial conditions. This might be contested by someone who thinks the initial conditions are in the antecedent, in this example, 'being rapidly immersed in water'. But this is incorrect. If it really is the regularity we want to explain, immersion in hot water appears in the *explanandum*, not in the *explanans*. The *explanans* must consist wholly in more general theories, each of which has the form of a universal. Consequently, not only does Hempel's model fail to capture these cases, these cases cannot admit of historical explanation on the definition. We have then a kind of explanation which is not historical as I have defined it, and the claim that the definition makes all explanations historical is seen to be false.

It may be valuable to say something about the place of the explanation of regularities in natural science. In general it has been assumed by philosophers of science, like Hempel and Oppenheim (and Salmon), that the explanation of natural events is an important part of the business of science. In recent years, however, this assumption has come under attack. In an interesting essay entitled 'The Place of the Explanation of Particular Facts in Science' W P Alston argues that the explanation of particular facts does not play a central role in pure science and hence that philosophers of science are misguided in supposing that the understanding of such explanations is one of the central tasks of the philosophy of science. He opens his argument with rather a nice fable:

Dr Wissenschaft, a well known research physicist, is relaxing over a cocktail before dinner, and Frau W says to him, 'You look awfully tired dear. Have a hard day at the lab?' 'Yes' the eminent doctor replies 'it was terribly exhausting, but I accomplished a great deal. I succeeded in explaining 250 cases of moisture forming on the outside of glasses when they were filled with iced water' (1: p. 14).

Alston wants to explain the obvious absurdity of this story and he does so, convincingly to my mind, by showing that the explanation of particular facts is *not* important in research physics or in any other theoretical science. But this conclusion does not put an end to *explanation* in science.

Let me hasten to add that I am not at all asserting that explanation is not central to pure science. On the contrary, explanation may without exaggeration be said to be its crowning achievement. But it is explanation of general nomological facts, not [explanation of particular facts] that occupies this position. Physics tries to explain phenomena of locomotion, expansion and electrical transmission; chemistry the rusting of metals and the souring of milk; psychology, differential rates of learning and depth perception. But the research physicist does not occupy himself with the explanation of the boiling of a particular kettle of water as such . . .; he is concerned to explain the nomological fact that water (under certain conditions) boils at 212°F (ibid: p. 18).

The combination of Alston's argument about science with mine about history has a number of interesting consequences. Some of these I shall take up later but at this point two are especially relevant. If, as I have argued, some of the natural sciences—geomorphology, evolutionary biology, parts of geology and cosmology for example—aim to explain particular events and matters of fact while others, those which interest Alston, do not, we need a distinction between and within the natural sciences which reflects this difference. Alston calls those sciences which are not concerned with the explanation of particular facts pure sciences, but this suggests a not altogether illuminating distinction with applied sciences, and following Popper we might do better to call them *theoretical* since this conveys something of their interest in generality. They may thus be contrasted with historical sciences which do seek to explain particular facts of the environment and natural history. If we add to this the observation that there is nothing wrong or misleading about continuing to call them sciences, we must conclude that the proper contrast is between theoretical and historical explanation, not between historical and scientific.

The terms 'historical' and 'theoretical' used in the way I have just specified meet both the conditions laid down in Chapter 2. In each case there is reason to classify an explanation in one way rather than the other and both descriptions tell us something about its character as an explanation. Neither of these conditions is satisfied by the expression 'scientific explanation' and despite its ubiquitousness, it is an expression which can be abandoned without loss. Moreover, to replace the traditional distinction with that between theoretical and historical explanations is to bring greater clarity to an area where there has been considerable confusion, though I have introduced it here chiefly to refute the suggestion that on my definition all explanations must turn out to be historical.

The distinction between theoretical and historical is not new, of course. It is to be found in Popper's celebrated essay *The Poverty of Historicism* and again in his *The Open Society and its Enemies*. But the distinction I want to draw is not quite the same as Popper's and perhaps it would be well to say wherein the differences lie and what their importance is.

Popper is committed to the Hempelian covering law model. Indeed he claims it for his own. His account of explanation is deductive and nomological therefore. He holds, that is to say, that to explain a fact is to deduce it from premises which contain at least one natural law or law-like regularity. Theoretical sciences seek to explain regularities by deducing them from other more general laws, while historical sciences explain individual events by deducing them from laws and statements of initial conditions. In both cases the explanations, according to Popper, are causal. It appears, then, that his distinction is closely tied to one model of explanation, as well as to the notion of causality. What I want to show is that the distinction I have drawn is not committed to the covering law model of explanation or even the hypothetico-deductive account of scientific inference in this way.

According to my definition a theoretical explanation is one which explains an observed regularity by reference to some more general theory and is to be contrasted with an historical explanation which explains some particular fact of its history. I deliberately use the vague expressions 'in terms of' and 'by reference to' because I cannot say, but do not need to say, precisely what the relation between *explanans* and *explanandum* is in either case. In the first part of his book *Laws and Explanation in History* Dray has arguments which purport to show that in many cases a nomological connection is quite insufficient to forge an explanatory relationship between an event and its explanation, and Salmon, in *Statistical Explanation and Statistical Relevance,* has arguments to show that explanations are not *arguments* at all. I find both of these pieces quite convincing and if they are right Popper and Hempel, clearly, must be wrong. But if they are, the distinction I have drawn is quite unaffected, for on my own account theoretical explanations may still be distinguished from historical ones whether or not the connection between *explanans* and *explanandum* is nomological or deductive. In other words Popper's belief that historians are law-takers while natural scientists are law-makers depends upon the truth of the claim that historical explanation no less than theoretical explanation employs general laws and it is in virtue of doing so that historical explanations explain. On my account, however, it is easy to distinguish historical and theoretical explanation even if appeal to general laws is neither a necessary nor a sufficient condition of explanation in either case.

It might be thought that though Popper's account of explanation in general cannot escape objections to the nomological model his distinction between the historical and the theoretical remains unaffected by these. But this is not quite right. It should be remembered that Popper's is a distinction between historical and theoretical *sciences*, the former exhibiting an interest in the discovery and explanation of singular matters of fact, the latter in the discovery and explanation of laws. Explanation is everywhere the same, that is, deductive and nomological. The difference is that the historical sciences are interested in the explanation of particular facts. Now if we recall my example of Jones's trip to the payroll office, the explanation given there will on Popper's view be historical, since it is the explanation of a particular event. But I argued that in fact we have no reason to describe it in this way. Even if we locate the *explanandum* event in the past, as Popper invariably does, we can easily conceive of explanations, even explanations which appear to fit the covering law model, which, if I am right, it would be a mistake to call historical. For instance, we might explain Sir Thomas More's refusal to approve Henry VIII's assumption of supreme governorship of the church of England by reference to his loyalty to Catholicism. This loyalty, since it endured both before and after his action, is not an event which preceded it. It does not, therefore, supply an historical explanation of his action on my definition. Just what sort of explanation it is, it is not my business to say. Or rather, just what predicate it would be useful or reasonable to apply to it depends upon issues which it would not be pertinent to raise now. But plainly, the fact that it does not have that feature which, I have claimed, would give us reason to call it historical while it is nonetheless the explanation of a particular event and an explanation of the sort that is common in the writing of political history entitles us to draw three important conclusions. First, it cannot be the case that all explanations in history are historical explanations. This may seem paradoxical but in fact it is nothing other than a statement of the obvious, and a proposition which even the staunchest opponents of the covering law model have had to concede when they have observed, with Dray, both that 'the explanations found in history books are a logically miscellaneous lot' (23: p. 85), and that it is the business of the historian to use whatever kind of explanation he may need for the task in hand. This is a point to which I shall return. Secondly, since the explanation of More's refusal is the explanation of a particular event and thus on Popper's view an historical one but not on mine, it serves to establish that the distinction I have drawn between theoretical and historical explanation is not the same as his between the theoretical and historical sciences. This is not, it is true, to adduce anything in the way of support for my view as against Popper's, but it does show at least that it is not merely an old and familiar one dressed up in new clothing. Thirdly, if the explanation of this particular fact is not historical as I have defined it then it cannot be that all explanations of particular events come out historical on my definition. Thus it provides a second refutation of the second objection I set out at the start.

3.   Let us turn to two objections which, in different ways, purport to show the worthlessness of the definition of historical explanation I have offered. The first of these claims to detect an important circularity and hence emptiness in it. The point may be made in the following fashion. Take the familiar case of explaining why the engine of my car has seized. The definition tells us that an historical explanation of this occurrence will point us to the event or events that preceded it. But of course, thus stated, it is quite inadequate. Events temporarily prior to the seizure are legion and even if we restrict ourselves to the relatively recent past and to events connected with the engine we still have a very large number. Amongst these, let us suppose, are the sump's being cracked, my having cleaned the plugs and the installation of a new air filter. It is with the first of these that the explanation lies but to refer to either of the other two events would, since it is reference to a preceding event, qualify as an historical explanation. We see, then, that the definition is deficient. It ought to read: an historical explanation of an event is one which refers us to *that part of the past which explains it.* Amplified in this way, it is plain that the definition employs the notion it is designed to explicate and once we add to this the observation that any reference to initial conditions must be reference to a fact temporally prior to that which is to be explained, we have uncovered the utterly trivial character of the claim. This triviality may be further illustrated by a parallel. Suppose that we are interested in the analysis of causal explanation and someone advises us that we need not become embroiled in the difficult question of

generality *v.* singularity because, he tells us, there is a clear, obvious and intelligible criterion of causal explanation available, namely, that a causal explanation is one which makes references to causes. Upon consideration we find that it is not reference to any old causes that is meant, but reference to explanatory causes, and hence that the question 'In virtue of what does reference to causes explain?' is left unanswered. We must surely consider ourselves cheated and the definition true, possibly, in virtue of a triviality which leaves everything as it is.

There is a short reply to this objection. My aim in this monograph has been to determine what it is that makes an historical explanation *historical*, not what makes it an explanation. Consequently, whatever conditions must be satisfied for a conjunction of propositions to constitute an explanation must be satisfied by any candidate for the title 'historical explanation'. But there are other conditions besides these, for we may also ask whether it is an historical one. My answer to this question is, that it is if it makes reference to the past, not if it does not, and I have been at pains to point out that not all explanations are historical by this definition. Despite the objection, then, the definition does what it is supposed to do, namely, pick out of the total class of explanations those that we have reason to call historical. Nor am I averse to the parallel with causal explanation. If we really are interested in what makes a causal explanation causal, I cannot see any better answer than the suggestion that such explanation consists in the attribution of causes. The truth is, of course, that those who set out to analyse causal explanation are not interested in this question at all but in the question, 'What makes the attribution of causes explanatory?'

I can imagine some dissatisfaction with this reply and a point of departure for further objection may be found in my last remark. If the analysis of causal explanation provides us with no clue as to what makes a causal explanation explanatory, not only does it have nothing to say on the question which has interested philosophers, it violates one of the two conditions I set down in Chapter 2 above, viz. that any qualification of 'explanation' must tell us something about its character as explanation. In point of fact this is incorrect. Both my definition of historical explanation and the suggested definition of causal explanation do tell us something along these lines: that the *explanans* must contain certain elements in each case, past events and causes.

But there is lurking here I think a more deep-seated objection. The parallel with causal explanation, after all, is not without force and what it shows is that no one can ignore completely the integrated character of expressions like 'historical explanation' and determine to pay attention to one half of them only. If he does, the fact that he is talking about explanation will be quite coincidental to what he has to say, for his claim is just that *anything* described as historical must have something to do with the past. Explanation drops out of the picture altogether. Fortunately the definition I have offered is able to overcome this objection. I think I can show that historical explanation as I have defined it describes a form of explanation with which we are familiar and, more importantly, gives us criteria by which to determine the satisfactoriness of explanations with this form.

We ought to observe first of all that the definition requires an historical explanation of some fact to refer to *its* past, not to *the* past. This enables us to deal fairly speedily with one aspect of the objection we are considering here as I first set it out. We are not helpless in the face of the fact that for any given event the events which preceded it are legion. Almost all of these are not parts of *its* history and we have only to deal with a relatively small number of preceding events. Even so it may be thought that the number is still embarrassingly large, so large in fact that the definition tells us nothing about which of these are actually to be gathered together to form anything approaching an explanation. In other words, since for any given event the historian must make a selection out of the events of its past in order to explain it, the definition cannot tell us what it is that makes the selection explanatory. For example, if his aim is to explain the French Revolution the number of events which comprise its past is so great that anything worthy of the name explanation must consist in a drastic reduction of these by selection.

But this example is badly chosen. 'The French Revolution' is a label for a vast concatenation of events and it would be implausible to think that there could be a simple and single explanation which would encompass them all. As a matter of fact 'The French Revolution' can reasonably be used to refer to major social and political events in France for any part of the time 1789–99 so that what appear on the surface to be competing accounts of the Revolution may be quite compatible. Indeed, just as an ambiguity over the precise nature of the *explanandum* confounds Hempel's account of explanation, so a good deal of confusion has attended the discussion of historical explanation because of failure to notice the importance of specifying precisely what it is that is to be explained. If we do specify the *explanandum* precisely we can see that in at least some cases the business of explaining a fact just is the business of discovering its history.

I can illustrate these points and their importance with an example whose length will be justified, I hope, by its interest. It is the strange death of Viscount Castlereagh, a politician whose career had been marked by the special importance each office took on as he came to occupy it. He had been Chief Secretary for Ireland at the time of the Act of Union, Secretary for War during the time of the Peninsular Campaign, and Foreign Secretary during the post-Napoleonic settlement of Europe. In 1822 he could look forward to still greater eminence and was in fact about to attend another important European conference in Verona when he took his own life. The explanation of his suicide was readily available and the inquest had plenty of evidence for and no difficulty in arriving at the verdict that he cut his own throat while mentally unbalanced. In the context of his abilities, position and likely future his death was a tragedy but suicide by the insane is a common enough occurrence and there is nothing about it which stands in need of special explanation. Furthermore, the explanation of his suicide, if I am right, is not an historical one for it refers us to a condition contemporaneous with his death and not to an event which preceded it. It might be cast in historical form, perhaps, by pointing to his going mad as the cause of his death, but this is somewhat factitious in my view because strictly speaking, since the first signs of insanity were observed a week to ten days before his death, it is his being mad rather than his going mad which explains it.

So far there is nothing to make his death a strange one. But circumstances, which emerged when a full account of it was in, disclosed elements which were a little more mysterious. I shall mention only three. First, he cut his throat with singular efficiency, so much so that he died within moments. Secondly, the knife he used was a common penknife never before seen in his possession. Thirdly, his delusion took the form of a conviction that everyone around him was conspiring to accuse him of having committed homosexual acts. The first point I want to make about this example is one I shall only mention briefly here and return to later on. It is that the elements in this death which stand in need of explanation run counter to our expectations. Were we to be told that very frequently those who commit suicide while insane are deluded about conspiracies to accuse them of the crime generally considered most heinous, or that all those who cut their own throats make neat and effective incisions, there would be nothing to explain about the appearance of these features in this particular death.[10] The elements which I have here described as mysterious would be mysterious no longer and prompt no search for explanation. The second point I have to make is that the need for an explanation has arisen because we have a much more precise description of the event to be explained than the expression 'the death of Castlereagh' supplies. The third point is that the explanation of these three elements is accomplished by the discovery of preceding events, as the facts show.

It was discovered with respect to the first puzzle that some years before Castlereagh had had dinner with a surgeon and inquired, perhaps idly, about the precise location of the jugular vein and the effect of its severance. With respect to the second, the evidence of a visitor to London who, having had Castlereagh pointed out to him in the street, determined to follow this great man for a time, showed that a few days before his death he had, apparently impulsively, purchased a penknife from a street trader. The third puzzle was resolved some years later when it emerged that Castlereagh had at least once, some three years before, accepted the advances of a prostitute and on entering the brothel discovered that the 'girl' was in fact a boy and that the event had been the result of a conspiracy to blackmail him. The first attempt at blackmail referred only to his traffic with prostitutes but the second, disclosed it appears in a letter he received shortly before his death, accused him of homosexuality, an accusation which had destroyed the Bishop of Clogher in a recent and celebrated scandal.

What this example and these explanations show is that once we are clear about what precisely we want to explain, the explanation lies in the history of those facts, that is, the relevant preceding events. The case of the knife illustrates this most clearly. It might be suggested, for example, that the facts about his coming to possess it do not adequately account for his having a knife which no one had seen him with before, since they do not tell us how he managed to hold on to it when his wife had been so careful to remove all razors and similar objects with which he might injure himself. But to argue this way is to seek the explanation of a fact different to that with which we began. What we now want to know is not how he came to have such a knife, but how he came to have it still. And the explanation of the latter no less than the former lies in a preceding event, though a different one, that he had, let us say, hidden it. In general, I am claiming, to have described the *explanandum* precisely is to be left in no doubt about which preceding event explains it.

If all this is right my definition of historical explanation describes a form of explanation which we have good reason to call historical and which in many cases is complete. What I mean by this is that my analysis of the explanation reduces the question of its adequacy to the question whether the *explanans* is true. If we allow that it is, we are entitled to conclude that the fact in question has been explained. This puts it at an advantage over Hempel's account since both elements of the 'explanation sketch' he allows an historian to produce may be true and we may still be left in doubt about its being an explanation. It might be thought that really there is no advantage here since the definition omits any account of the *connection* between *explanans* and *explanandum* and hence no account of how one explains the other. But this objection is out of order for two reasons. First, as Hume showed, if, past a certain point, we insist upon being given a connection between a fact and its explanation we open the way to an infinite regress, because whatever we choose as a suitable connection, are we not entitled then to look for something to connect the fact and the connection? Secondly, the sorts of cases I have been discussing are clearly past this point. If it is suggested that, faced with the fact of Castlereagh's having bought the knife as an explanation of his possessing it, we can still ask whether his buying it really explains his having it, there can be no end to such questions. This is a point to which I shall return in the concluding chapter.

We may conclude, then, that historical explanation as I have defined it constitutes a form of explanation whose explanatory character no less than its historical character is encompassed in the definition. Once we have stated precisely what it is we want to explain its explanation very often lies in its history and when this is the case there is only one way in which explanations of this kind can be faulted, by the *explanans* being false. It cannot fail by being incomplete. Sometimes this may appear to be the case but the fault often lies, as we have seen, with too imprecise a definition of the *explanandum*. Where the explanandum is precisely described and the facts adduced are true and relevant, they cannot lack explanatory force, for any further demand of this sort is unintelligible.

I should like to turn aside from the main burden of the argument for a moment in order to amplify my claim that the place of generalisations and truisms in historical explanation very often lies not as has been thought in the provision of explanations but in the determination of what stands in need of explanation. Consider this example. It has been widely supposed that Richard III was responsible for the murder of the Princes in the Tower. This supposition casts a very curious light on the behaviour of the Queen Dowager who appears to have attended and allowed her daughters to attend festivities at court and to have accepted a generous pension from Richard very shortly after the murders are said to have taken place. As the historian Sir Cuthbert Oliphant wrote,

> The conduct of the Queen Dowager is hard to explain; whether she feared to be taken from sanctuary by force, or whether she was merely tired of her forlorn existence at Westminster and had resolved to be reconciled to the murderer of her two sons out of mere callous apathy seems uncertain.

Now why should we think that we need an explanation in this case? The answer that it is natural to give is that her behaviour is contrary to that which we should expect from the mother of sons who have been murdered towards their murderer. It is this belief in the truth of a generalisation which we could formulate that creates the difficulty.

Suppose that psychologists furnish us with a law which shows that under a more refined description the conduct of the Dowager is true to form. We can say if we wish that they have explained her behaviour (and their explanations fit the Hempelian pattern) but it seems equally plausible, and in my view more natural, to say that in this case there is nothing special to be explained. Which we say will depend, I think, upon the extent to which the law they adduce contradicts our common beliefs. If it is contrary to what we commonly believe we shall be more inclined to say that they have explained her behaviour; if it is a law which we had all supposed to have held, we shall say that her behaviour was not odd after all. If the former holds true, it is worth noticing that the explanation of which we are now possessed is a psychological not an historical one and one that the historian as such is in no special position to provide.

These judgements about the place of psychological laws in the explanation of behaviour are slightly doubtful perhaps but they are lent some support by being contrasted with the impact of strictly historical inquiry which shows that Richard III did not murder the princes or have them done to death. Immediately the Dowager's behaviour is recast into the actions of a woman towards a powerful relative. You can say, if you like, that her behaviour is now explained, or that it needs no explanation. The point is that, either way, the impact of historical investigation is the same as psychology, without employing generalisations in the way that psychology does.

I want to close my discussion of the third objection by turning to the suggestion that my account of historical explanation is only a repetition of what others have said, perhaps better, about the important place of narrative in history. It is hardly a criticism of philosophical argument that it is not novel, but it must be allowed that without some measure of novelty an argument loses its interest. However, in this case, I am glad to say, the charge is ill-founded, because 'narrative' is a much more complex notion than 'historical explanation'. The history in which I have said historical explanation consists comprises a single event whereas narrative typically is the story of a sequence of events. Furthermore a decent narrative must include elements like character, beliefs, dispositions and so on, which could not be preceding events and are thus excluded from an historical explanation as I have defined it. On a brief consideration we can thus detect at least two features which distinguish historical narrative and historical explanation.

This reply may prompt the thought, however, that if historical explanation is not narrative and on these grounds, it is a very uninteresting creature indeed. This brings me to the fourth and final objection listed at the start.

4.   In the previous two chapters it was my constant complaint that philosophers have not paid enough attention to questions about the *historical* character of historical explanation, despite express avowals on the part of some of them to pay attention to what historians actually do. In the course of the argument we were led to reject the common assumption that historical explanations are peculiarly explanations of human actions or affairs, and hence the view that history proper is human history and that anything called natural history is at best peripheral. There is likely to be some question about how widely the view I have seen fit to reject has actually been held. I have documented its prevalence as best I can without unduly burdening the argument. But to someone who raises this point such documentation may not count for very much, for I have no doubt his suspicion will be that I have lent a sharpness and rigidity to the remarks one may find philosophers making which foist upon them doctrines to which they do not subscribe. In other words there may be a feeling that the true character of most philosophers' distinctions between history and nature has been misrepresented in what I have said so that my arguments are not of much consequence in the context of what people actually believe. Besides, there is likely to be a residual dissatisfaction with any account of historical explanation which, like mine, has historical explanation making an appearance in sciences of a radically different nature, since this so massively fails to tell us anything about the peculiarities of history as it is generally understood, and in which philosophers, without exception almost, have been interested. I am unsure how much weight to give to this dissatisfaction. My definition has implications which run counter to a very deeply held assumption, but if the arguments have been sound I have succeeded in defining historical explanation in a way which shows both its historical and its explanatory character and I do not know that there is anything left to do. But because the dissatisfaction is almost certain to be felt, it may be valuable to set out the objection in its strongest light and see what there is to be said.

We should not be deceived by the examples I have been using in the last few pages into thinking that historical explanation is peculiarly important in the history of human affairs. It is easy to demonstrate that what I have said about it applies equally well to the explanation of natural phenomena. Consider, for example, the problem of the 'Cambrian explosion' in evolutionary theory. The fossil record shows, apparently, that prior to the Cambrian period single-celled organisms had existed for between 2000 and 3000 million years but that in the relatively short period of 200 million years, and especially in the last 50 million of these, a host of different and complex creatures came into existence. How is the 'explosion' of multicellular forms to be explained? One theory is that the fossil record is just misleading and that throughout the Precambrian gradual development took place but in restricted localities or where fossilisation was unlikely. Another is that the fossil record is as it is because of an explosion of creative activity during the relevant period. The explosion is in turn explained by the theory that oxygen concentration only reached a level high enough to support active multicellular animals in the late Precambrian. On my definition the second of these is an historical explanation; it explains the fossil record by referring us to what happened and it explains what happened by reference to what happened before that. I do not know what plausibility is to be attributed to this theory and of course the time scale is rather longer than that with which historians usually operate, but nevertheless it is clearly a possible explanation and one which explains by referring us to a relevant preceding event. In short, then, some explanations in the evolutionary sciences are historical.

To those who are troubled by the objection I have here set myself to consider, the fact that my account of historical explanation applies to natural events will be readily conceded. This is part of their complaint no doubt, but not the main part. For, they will argue, the idea that the natural past can be investigated and explained, that nature has a past, is not worth disputing since there is an obvious sense in which it is true. What *is* worth disputing is whether the minimal definition of 'historical' I have given and which clearly encompasses both nature and society is the whole sense that normally attaches to that word: whether, that is to say, there is not a distinctive kind of explanation which we have reason to call historical, rather richer than mine and one more in keeping with the thoughts and arguments of some of those I have attacked. And the suggestion that there is may be strengthened once we draw attention to the following sorts of case. First, there are many occasions in the study of human history when explanation by reference to a preceding event would just be insufficient. For example, no historian could rest content with explaining the outbreak of the American Civil War by reference to the ordinance of secession which followed Lincoln's election to the Presidency in 1860 or, perhaps more immediately, to the attack on Fort Sumter in April 1861. Before the consequences of these events can be made intelligible we need to be told not merely what happened but about the relationship between North and South which had grown up. Secondly, there are cases where an historical explanation as I have defined it seems to be impossible but where explanation is nonetheless required. For instance, in 1882 Gladstone, who was then Prime Minister, ordered the use of military force to assist the Khedive in the suppression of an Egyptian nationalist uprising. But in 1885, faced with an equally nationalistic uprising against the same ruler, this time in the Sudan, he went to considerable lengths to avoid the use of force against the rebels, arguing that theirs was the expression of a legitimate aspiration to freedom, a policy which led in the end to one of the most famous episodes of the century, the death of General Gordon. How are we to explain this inconsistency? If an event is to be adduced to explain it (like his having second thoughts or changing his mind) it must be an event occurring *between* the two occasions with which we are concerned and cannot therefore be an event preceding that which we wish to explain.[10] In any case the evidence shows that it is to be explained not in the light of any one event but in the light of Gladstone's aims and beliefs, his conception of politics and the characteristic workings of his mind. In short, what is required is that we make the two actions intelligible from the point of view of the agent, however odd that point of view may be to us.

Plainly we have here a form of explanation which requires appeal to the minds of historical agents, which appeal gathers the events together into an intelligible sequence, a narrative of the past. It is this form of agent explanation, it will be said, in which philosophers of history, especially of Collingwood's stripe, have been interested chiefly, and their reason for calling it historical is that it involves appeal to an historically located point of view. Furthermore, it seems right to deny that it shares any common feature with explanation in historical geology or biology.

In reply I should say at the outset that I have no doubt that narrative of the sort here described forms a large part, if not the mainstay, of the history of human affairs. All I wish to assert is that, though by calling it historical we may mislead very few, this description is not incontestable in the way that my definition is because it does not pick out some indisputable peculiarity of the history of human affairs. My reason for thinking this is that explanatory narrative is not confined to nor the prerogative of the historian but is also the principal way in which novels and dramas are constructed and made intelligible to the reader. If it is replied to this point that narratives in novels and the like precisely masquerade as what might have been (but are not) bits of history, this begs the question. Besides it is not obviously true. *The Lord of the Rings* makes use of narrative in order to make the sequence of events intelligible to the reader, but there is no plain sense in which this might have been a piece of history. The fact is that what is revealed to us by attention to the explanatory power of narrative is the character of what we might, for the sake of a name, call drama, rather than the character of history, and not all dramas are historical. Consequently, to insist that in narrative we have uncovered the nature of historical explanation amounts to saying that there is nothing distinctive to be marked off in this way at all.

There may be some resistance to this argument, resulting perhaps from the belief that if it is not strictly accurate to describe dramas as possible histories at least both history and drama are narrative in a way that natural 'histories' could not be. The idea is this. A story has, roughly, a beginning, a middle and an end, and these divisions mark the relative significance of the events within it. Now significance is something which arises in connection with the point of a story, its meaning for the agents involved and for those who tell it, and 'meaning' is just what cannot be attributed to natural events. A natural history is, no doubt, a connected sequence of events but one event in the sequence does not have any peculiar significance in virtue of the sequence in which it appears. It is just there. We can see a general recognition of this difference reflected, it might be said, in one use of the word 'historic' as it is applied to social and political events, even individual actions, and as it cannot be applied to natural events. A constitutional reform or the decision of a general in battle may in this sense be said to be historic, but an earthquake or the eruption of a volcano could not. And it is this sense of the historic that the assimilation of human and natural history overlooks and by doing so leaves everything that is important to the philosopher of history out of account.

This is of course a familiar line of thought. Perhaps I should emphasise that nothing for which I have argued carries the implication that the natural and human sciences are indistinguishable in every particular nor that the whole range of kinds of explanation available to one is available to the other. Indeed I incline to the view, contrary to Hempel's, that there is a radical difference between human action and natural events which no serious study of human behaviour can ignore and that failure to acknowledge this is partly what renders Skinner's psychology, for instance, so empty. But be this how it may, and whether I am right or wrong, the argument I have just set out does nothing to disturb the claim that geologists, geomorphologists and biologists are engaged in history in more than a minimal sense, because they can certainly produce narratives of the course of natural history. The natural no less than the human past is, after all, a continuous sequence of indefinitely many events and in order to narrate or explain anything whatever some drastic selection is necessary. Each natural history, therefore, selects out of the totality, those events that truly have a bearing upon the object of the inquiry. Setting out these events is just what the basis of any natural history consists in and each event is given a significance precisely in virtue of its relation to the given end which we seek to explain. It is therefore quite in order to speak of the significance of a natural event, and the more far-reaching its consequences in the wider area of inquiry, the greater its significance. Thus the increase in the proportion of oxygen in the atmosphere, on one explanation of the Cambrian explosion mentioned above, is an event of great significance. Of course just *how* one event has a bearing on the end to be explained will differ not just from subject to subject but from one case to another and it certainly seems that there are ways in which one action may bear upon another which could not be a way in which natural events were related—a flood could not be the realised intention of a landslide—though it is a familiar enough suggestion that the connection between intention and actualisation is ultimately causal no less than that between landslide and flood. All that needs to be emphasised here, however, is that we need, and have, an idea of the relative significance of different natural events in a sequence which makes narrative possible in natural history. What we may not have is any sense of the *meaning* of a natural event (leaving aside the purposes of God) but nothing in the argument I have been considering shows that to be essential and the unargued move from significance to meaning is illicit.

The kind of explanatory narrative which has caught the attention of a number of philosophers of history, then, is not peculiar to history. Neither is it restricted to human history nor indeed common to all branches of human history. I see no reason to deny that a geomorphologist can tell the story of, say, Lake Superior. He tells us, after all, what happened in the past, not to the towns and the people in the area but to the land form itself over the last 500 million years, so that it came to be as it is. Moreover, he is and must be concerned to discover the important and the unimportant amongst all that happened during that period. What he produces is a telescoped and abstracted but connected narrative of events. I suspect it would be right to endorse the claim made against the covering law model that the connections between these events will be of a quite different order from those between, say, one action of Gladstone's and another, but it does not follow that the history of Lake Superior is not a narrative history, or somehow less than real history. For while it may be true that explanatory narrative invoking the self-understanding of agents, their intentions, purposes, beliefs and aspirations, is of the greatest importance in biography, political, military and ecclesiastical history, it is less clear that this is true of social and economic history which are nonetheless concerned with human affairs. In particular it is not true of 'invisible hand' explanations (see 32: pp. 18–22) which concern the actions of individuals and the unintended macroeffects of their interaction. Besides, it is impossible to deny that even in the most individualised history natural events can play a part. The death of Alexander the Great, for instance, did create circumstances which other agents had to perceive, understand and react to, but more simply it also removed one factor in the development of Greece.

As these remarks imply, I do not believe that there is any striking unity in the study of history, at the level of explanation and understanding. This is not just because somewhat quirkishly I insist upon calling natural history history, but because different branches of the history of human affairs must also proceed differently. I do not even believe that there is any special unity in the understanding and explanation of human actions. I offer instead a definition of historical explanation which has a unity in virtue of what it says and the fact that we can, if we wish, use it to pick out a distinctive class of explanations. It has the drawback that it turns out not to be very interesting, at least to some minds, because it shows that the questions about the nature of historical explanation can be settled very simply and the really difficult problems are to be found in the philosophy of action. A proper perception of this point would no doubt lead many students and teachers to abandon the philosophy of history altogether since it is so obvious that their interest has really lain in the understanding and explanation of action not in the nature of historical inquiry. But even if they are right in this, there is still something to be gained from a correct understanding of the points that truly concern history. Most obviously there is the clarification which we may bring to the debate between the covering law theorists and their opponents. But there are other benefits too and it is to these that I now turn.

6

Some implications

It would be foolish to suppose that having answered four objections I have laid all possible doubts and difficulties about my account of historical explanation to rest. I am well aware that other criticisms may be brought against it and that some of these are to be found in the writings of those I have myself criticised. Nevertheless there comes a point past which it is tedious to pursue the issue in this rather negative way and I should like instead to outline some positive advantages to construing historical explanation along the lines I suggest. To this end it may be valuable to summarise the conclusions I take to have been established.

If our subject is historical explanation we cannot hope to settle philosophical questions which arise concerning it and at the same time disregard the normal uses of the words 'history' and 'historical' or the facts of historical inquiry as it has been pursued. Conversely, however, it is a mistake to think that these questions can be settled solely by reference to what historians do or simply by describing what we find in history books, because there is too much uncertainty about which are the relevant facts and how they are to be weighed into the argument. Since neither alternative is wholly satisfactory we must look instead for a clear, obvious and intelligible criterion of historical explanation; and in fact there is one readily at our disposal, the proposition that an historical explanation is one which explains a fact by giving its history. Upon investigation this turns out to involve the discovery of a relevant preceding event. A proper grasp of this criterion shows it to be a mistake to draw a strong distinction, at least as far as explanation is concerned, between the natural and the human sciences. Rather a more valuable distinction is to be drawn between historical and theoretical explanation. Once this is clear we can see that a satisfactory characterisation of historical explanation does not involve the question whether the explanation of human action is or is not assimilable to any given model of explanation in general. The further implications of this criterion I shall now consider in turn, as I have done the objections to it.

1. The first implication is that 'explanation in history', where this expression is taken to refer to the explanations we find in history books, is not the same as historical explanation. I agree with Dray that the explanations we find in history books are a pretty mixed bag and that historians must employ whatever explanations they need in order to make their narrative intelligible. Indeed I have given examples designed to show that psychological and dispositional explanations are to be found in and are a necessary part of many historical narratives. In other words historical explanation is only one kind of explanation that historians may have occasion to employ and furthermore, *pace* Ball, I see no reason to think that those who are not engaged in the study of history as we normally understand it, lawyers, journalists, art critics and so on, may not offer and employ historical explanations. The advantages of a divorce between 'historical explanation' and 'explanation in history' are considerable. We need no longer bother about conflict between the two. The work of historians can certainly be used to illustrate historical explanation but no purpose is served by bandying counterexamples and comparing impressions about what we should say of them. At the same time as freeing philosophical argument from dubious appeals to history books we also escape the dangers of legislating *a priori* about what historians do or ought to do. If I am right we have found reason to call a certain sort of explanation historical, but the historian is perfectly at liberty to reach for whatever form of explanation will suit his purposes. By the same token, the criterion does not rest upon any claims as to what is 'essential' or 'typical' or 'characteristic' in the works of historians and no half-hearted empirical survey is called for. Independence of each other is thus established for both history and philosophy, an independence which anyone who has witnessed historians' attempts to settle philosophical questions on the basis of their familiarity with the discipline or philosophers' attempts to lay down the law for historians must surely regard as desirable. Yet all contact between philosophy and the study of history is not lost since the criterion depends upon an obvious, and possibly necessary, connection between history and the past, that same connection which makes it absurd to suppose that an historian could be true to his trade and study the future.

2. The second major advantage that I claim for my account is that it puts genuine explanation within the proper province of the historian, and

does so in a way that shows once more the confused character of the
debate between the covering law theorists and their opponents. Both
sides to this debate suppose that explanations of particular facts have
three elements, the *explanandum* which we may call 'E', the initial
conditions 'C', and some link between the two, 'L'. The covering law
theorists argue that 'L' must be an empirical law of some sort so that
explanation consists in subsumption under law—i.e. this happened
because (under certain conditions) this *always* happens. Their opponents
have two principal objections. First, when we explain E by citing some C,
where E is an action, we explain E if and only if we make it *intelligible* by
citing C, and the truth of any generalisation 'whenever C then E' is
neither a necessary nor a sufficient condition of this. So, for instance, I
shall not have explained Bismarck's action of altering the Ems telegram
by the fact that he first picked up a red pencil, even if it is true (which it
might be) that the vast majority or even all of those who receive tele-
grams the wording of which they proceed to alter have first picked up a
red pencil. Secondly, if it were true that the provision of true empirical
generalisations is a necessary condition of explaining particular facts, it
would follow that the historian who, *qua* historian, is not the investi-
gator or possessor of such generalisations, does not supply any explanation but only constructs, at best, an explanation sketch. But it is absurd
to suppose that historians never explain at all. Both of these objections
are telling, it seems to me, though at least one conclusion that has been
drawn from this fact does not follow. It is, that what is needed to link C
and E in a satisfactory manner is a principle of action or reason, a
general belief on the part of the agent that in the circumstances C the
thing to do is E, which belief derives from the place of his action in a
pattern and context of conduct which he recognises. In defending this
claim heavy emphasis is usually placed on making the action intelligible
and no doubt this emphasis has been salutary, but even so the 'principle
of action' story is not very satisfactory because either it takes for granted
the kind of explanation involved or it leaves an important gap between C
(and L) and E. Donald Davidson has expressed the difficulty with the
following example (of Melden's):

> A man driving an automobile raises his arm in order to signal. His intention, to
> signal, explains his action, raising his arm, by redescribing it as signalling.
> What is the pattern that explains the action? Is it the familiar pattern of an
> action done for a reason? Then it does indeed explain the action, but only
> because it assumes the relation of reason and action that we want to analyse.
> Or is the pattern rather this: the man is driving, he is approaching a turn; he
> knows he ought to signal; he knows how to signal, by raising his arm. . . .
> Perhaps, as Melden suggests, if all this happens he does signal. And the

explanation would be this; if, under these conditions, a man raises his arm, then he signals. The difficulty is, of course, that this explanation does not touch the question of why he raised his arm. He had a reason to raise his arm but this has not been shown to be the reason why he did it. If the description 'signalling' explains his action by giving his reason, then the signalling must be intentional; but, on the account just given, it may not be (22: p. 10–11).

We see then, that there must be some other way of getting from C to E. But according to Davidson (and rightly in my view) the answer does not lie with generalisation. This is because

we are usually far more certain of a singular causal connection than we are of any causal law governing the case; does this show that Hume was wrong in claiming that singular causal statements entail laws? Not necessarily, for Hume's claim ['we may define a cause to be an object followed by another, and where all the objects similar to the first are followed by objects similar to the second'] is ambiguous. It may mean that 'A caused B' entails some particular law involving predicates used in the descriptions 'A' and 'B', or it may mean that 'A caused B' entails that there exists a causal law instantiated by some true descriptions of A and B. Obviously, both versions of Hume's doctrine give a sense to the claim that singular causal statements entail laws, and both sustain the view that causal explanations 'involve laws'. But the second version is far weaker, in that no particular law is entailed by a singular causal claim, and a singular causal claim can be defended, if it needs defence, without defending any law. Only the second version of Hume's doctrine can be made to fit with most causal explanations; it suits rationalisations equally well (ibid: p. 16–17).

Davidson's claim that singular causal statements may entail without being dependent upon generalisations is strengthened by the observation that the ability even to formulate a generalisation which could have explanatory value depends upon our making and being able to make singular explanatory statements and it is a claim, furthermore, which is plainly in accordance with the fact that, on my definition, historical explanation does not require us to move away from the investigation of singular matters of fact. Davidson, of course, wants to analyse particular rationalisations into singular statements of cause and effect and in this sense his arguments may seem to sustain more of the Hempelian theory of explanation than at first appears. His argument is that 'cause and effect form the sort of pattern that explains the effect in a sense of "explain" that we understand as well as any. If reason and action illustrate a different pattern of explanation, that pattern must be identified' (ibid: p. 10). This is rather a weak stopping point for it seems open to the proponents of rational explanation, who deny that it is causal, to hold that reason and action do form a pattern that explains, in a sense of 'explain' that we understand as well as any.

But who is right here does not matter for the purposes of the definition of historical explanation. The conclusion of Davidson's arguments relevant to our present concern is that we must be able to identify explanations that involve nothing more than the establishment of singular matters of fact. This is especially important in the case of history because the three element model of explanation invites us to construe explanation as something that takes place once all the facts are in. Thus the historian, for instance, is pictured as having to decide which out of a number of initial conditions that are shown to have been present is the true explanation of E. But in fact it is evident that historians rather rarely seek to explain historical puzzles by picking and choosing between sets of facts which have long been established and more commonly conceive of themselves as explaining *by* establishing the historical facts. Consider in illustration of this J C Beaglehole's explanation of the death of Captain Cook. This is an instructive piece because both in the elaboration of his own explanation and in his examination of one or two other contenders, Beaglehole argues in a way quite in keeping with the point I have been making.

The puzzle about Captain Cook's death is probably well known. It centres around the extraordinary reversal of his position amongst the South Sea islanders within a very short period of time. In January 1779 Cook put into Kealakekua Bay on the western side of the island of Hawaii. He was at once the recipient of divine honours and granted the use of a religious enclosure for his tents. His officers and men were popular, could explore wherever they wished with perfect safety and were aided in every way by the people. The ship left again at the beginning of February but bad weather and the need for repairs forced them back after only five days. Two days later the same islanders who had hailed Cook as the God Lono, killed him. Beaglehole examines several possible explanations, first that

> the class structure of Hawaii was one of chiefs, priesthood, and commoners, the last oppressed and exploited as commoners have always been. Cook came and was hailed as a god, by a priesthood always alive to the main chance; his presence played into their hands and vast quantities of provisions were virtually extorted from a groaning populace to feed not simply the stomachs of alleged deities, but the prestige of their professional servants. Naturally in due course when the oppressed ones saw the gods at a disadvantage they rose; and Cook, having accepted undue and unexpected exaltation incurred a just-as-little-expected retribution (40: pp. 290–291).

This explanation, could without much effort be cast into the form preferred by Hempel or by Dray. It obviously depends upon either generalisations or principles of action common to classes over a much wider

context than eighteenth-century Hawaii. But Beaglehole treats it in a way
that is true to the character of historical investigation as I have described
it by claiming that 'the trouble with this theory is that there is no evidence
to support it'. He proceeds to discount it not on the grounds that the relevant events are unsatisfactorily connected, but because it rests upon
claims which are false, since, for example, Cook's supplies of food were
not a forced tribute but bought in fair trade. The same is true of a second
possible explanation of the event, the suggestion that Cook was guilty of
a monstrous affront to Hawaiian religion by dismantling a paling inter-
spersed with religious images for firewood on board ship. But again in
the case of this explanation *not* all the facts are in, for it appears that
neither this sort of fence nor any image that formed part of it was
regarded by Hawaiians as sacred; either could be burnt.

The general point which is to be illustrated by this example is that
where, as in the case, we can plainly see the examination of alternative
explanations being undertaken, it is a mistake to think that all the facts
are given and that the difference between explanations lies in the way
they connect the facts. In fact, deciding between different explanations
just is a matter of settling the facts. When Beaglehole finally offers his
own explanation it too simply satisfies his own aim, 'to make our simple
tale really intelligible', by disclosing the essential facts of what happened
and the circumstances in which the event occurred.

3.   The third major implication of my suggestion about historical
explanation concerns the social sciences. A large part of the interest in
the question whether historical explanation has the same form as, or is
only a pointer to, or is an applied case of explanation in the natural
sciences arises from the question whether the social sciences, which
obviously deal in large part with the same subject matter as human
history, can or ought to be pursued in the same manner as physics or
chemistry. Now I have argued that historical explanation is to be found
in the natural sciences no less than in the study of human affairs and that
there is no interesting distinction to be made between historical and
scientific explanation, or indeed between the explanation of the natural
and the explanation of the social. Instead we should draw a distinction
between historical and theoretical explanation, and this naturally has
consequences for our view of the social sciences. Theoretical explanation, it will be recalled, is the explanation of observed regularities in
terms of theories, as for example, the generalities of Boyle's law and
Dalton's law are explained by the kinetic theory of gases. If this is true,
the first task of the theoretical scientist must be to isolate the regularities
which need to be explained. If there are none of these there is no scope

for theoretical explanation. Consequently, in so far as the social sciences are theoretical, that is, generalising inquiries, they must not only be productive of laws but also of regularities which those laws explain.

It is common to find philosophers arguing that, strictly speaking, social *science* is impossible because social phenomena are the outcome of human actions, it is reasons not causes that must be invoked in the explanation of action and hence social behaviour cannot be explained in terms of causal laws. This is a view which has influenced a good deal of the practice of social science as well as philosophical opinion concerning it, but if I am right the argument is not a good one. It may be true that we cannot explain the actions of an individual without appealing to his reasons and that this is at odds with any causal explanation (though I am not sure that this *is* true) but if the social sciences are or aim to be theoretical they will not in any case be concerned to explain the actions of individuals, but rather observed regularities in the behaviour of sets of individuals. And, if this is their aim, the truth of the claim about action, reasons and causes, does not matter very much because it needs to be shown independently that something of the same restriction holds good for patterns in social behaviour. The explanation of migratory patterns, for example, if there is one, could not consist in a summation of the individuals' reasons for migrating since this would do nothing to explain the pattern. Again, an individual might have very good reasons for voting in the way he does, but the explanation of his action will not set us on the road to explaining such regularities as there may be between, say, class membership and voting habits. Such constraints as we may have to observe in the explanation of human action, therefore, are not automatically constraints upon the possibility of procedures of the social sciences even though their subject matter is the social.

To be clear about the objects of explanation in the social sciences, however, in its turn produces other obstacles in the way of declaring that social science is an unproblematic enterprise, because there may be a serious limit to the number of regularities that we can supply for explanation. This is not just another way of saying, what is true I think, that as a matter of fact there are very few well attested regularities which social study has uncovered and that these are drawn from a data base drastically limited in spatial and temporal extent, but of drawing attention to a possible conceptual limit upon generalising about social phenomena. This is an issue discussed by Alasdair MacIntyre in his essay, 'Is a Science of Comparative Politics Possible?' In this essay he examines attempts to establish cross-cultural (and this means across different periods as well as different places) regularities in political behaviour and concludes that over certain ranges of behaviour it is impossible to generalise across cultures without violating the criteria of what is to count as the same phenomenon, just because those criteria are themselves determined by and relative to individual cultures. The problem is that having made a tentative generalisation 'the provision of an environment sufficiently different to make the search for counterexamples interesting will normally be the provision of an environment where we cannot hope to find examples of the original phenomenon and therefore cannot hope to find counterexamples' (12: p. 266).

It would take me too far beyond the proper scope of this monograph to examine his arguments in support of this claim. Besides, MacIntyre is expressly concerned with political science and the position may be different in other areas of social study. Indeed he himself seems to think it possible that we should produce true generalisations about human rationality which are not, however, part of any specifically political science but, I suppose, part of social psychology. Be this as it may, the implication I claim to find in my distinction between historical and theoretical explanation bears out MacIntyre's contention that before we can settle whether it is possible to produce social scientific theories, we must settle whether there are any facts, i.e. observed regularities in human behaviour for them to explain. And this, rather than the causality of human actions, is the major challenge and the chief stumbling block to the progress and development of social science.

4.   Another advantage which springs from my distinction between theoretical and historical explanation is that it provides a way in which we can avoid a problem that Hempel and others have had with the statistical explanation of particular facts. It is this. Explanation and prediction on Hempel's account both have the same form, basically

$$\frac{\text{All } F \text{ are } G}{x \text{ is } F}$$
$$x \text{ is } G$$

Where the law like statement to be employed is probabilistic, the form of the resulting statistical explanation must be expressible as follows:

$$\frac{\text{Almost all } F \text{ are } G}{x \text{ is } F}$$
$$x \text{ is almost certain to be } G$$

But though there appears to be a similarity here, in fact there is a fundamental difference between the two kinds of argument. As Hempel puts it:

Suppose, for example, that almost all, but not quite all penicillin-treated, streptococcal infections result in quick recovery, or briefly, that almost all P are R; and suppose also that the particular case of illness of patient John Jones which is under discussion—let us call it j—is an instance of P. Our original statistical explanation may then be expressed in the following manner, which exhibits the form above.

Almost all P are R
j is P
_____
j is almost certain to be R (8.3a)

Next, let us say that an event has the property P^* if it is either the event j itself or one of those infrequent cases of penicillin-treated streptococcal infection which do not result in quick recovery. Then clearly j is P^*, whether or not j is one of the cases resulting in recovery, i.e. whether or not j is R. Furthermore, almost every instance of P^* is an instance of non-R (the only possible exception being j itself). Hence, the argument (8.3a) in which, on our assumption, the premises are true can be matched with another one whose premises are equally true, but which by the very logic underlying (8.3a), leads to a conclusion which appears to contradict that of (8.3a):

Almost all P^* are non-R
j is P^*
_____
j is almost certain to be non-R (8: p. 126)

It might be protested that the counterexample involves an essential reference to particular individuals (such as j in this case) but Hempel has further argument which shows that the reference to a particular individual can be eliminated. He is left then with a very serious problem, for it seems that where statistical laws are involved in the deductive model of explanation, and he insists that 'there can be no question that statistical generalisations are widely invoked for predictive purposes in such diverse fields as physics, genetics and sociology' (ibid: p. 127), any information we can employ to predict or explain a particular occurrence can as easily be used to predict or explain its opposite.

Hempel finds a solution, or part of one, in the observation that the conclusions of the argument are not self-contained complete statements but elliptically formulated statements of a relational character, i.e. they are relative to the premises of the argument in which they appear. In this way the 'incompatible' conclusions become compatible because, taken relationally, they are not contradictory.

Now the point I want to make is that this solution, whether or not it is ultimately satisfactory, is plausible in the case of expectation and prediction but utterly implausible in the case of explanation. It is reasonable to think that contrary predictions can still be rational predictions given different bases, that is, that they can be compatible in advance of R, but it is much more difficult to see that the fact of R can in any way be explained by the likelihood of non-R, or even the likelihood of R if, as Hempel's argument shows, the likelihood of R can on available evidence be construed as being no greater than the likelihood of non-R. That nothing of this sort will serve to explain is evident from an examination of another example Hempel uses in the same place, the urn filled with black and white balls. Given a certain distribution of balls, say 99 black to 1 white, it is reasonable to expect and to predict that, for any draw, the ball drawn will be black. And we can still declare this to be the reasonable thing to predict even if it turns out that a white ball is drawn. But in what sense could the high probability of a black ball's being drawn explain the fact that a white ball *has* been drawn? It does not even explain why a black ball *rather than* a white one is drawn, when it is. What is needed, indeed the only thing possible in the way of explanation of these instances, is an historical explanation as I have defined it. The explanation of my drawing a white ball lies with the fact that it was upon a white ball that I put my hand inside the urn. If this seems rather tame and we ask in turn for *its* explanation, again an historical explanation is the only one that can be given, this time one in terms of the angle of my arm and the position of the ball—perhaps that it was on the top. In short, nothing about the particular case can be explained by appealing to probabilities and since these are the only law-like statements which might occupy the place of major premise in the argument form, we must conclude that there is something wrong with Hempel's whole treatment of statistical explanation.

It might be thought that there is nonetheless something which the probabilities do explain, namely the relative frequency of black and white balls over a number of draws. In fact Hempel argues that here too the problem of what he calls the ambiguity of statistical formulation arises. I think he is right in this, but in any case there is a further objection to invoking probabilities in explanation in this way. The probability, after all, is a probability for drawings from the urn and, at least on the frequency interpretation of probability which is a plausible one in this case, this means that any attempt at this sort of explanation would be an attempt to explain the frequency by appeal to the very same frequency. In fact, in the example envisaged, the frequency is actually explained by the relative distribution of balls in the urn, that is by a statement of fact about the urn, not a statement of probabilities. This illustrates an important point. The relative frequency of black and white balls is a regularity in the sense in which I spoke of theoretical explanations seeking to explain observed regularities, and such regularities are not uncommon in the natural sciences, as for instance, in certain observations about the rate of destruction for atoms of uranium. But in the urn case the explanation lies with a 'theory' about what we might call the structure of the urn and this suggests that the theories in terms of which theoretical explanations explain need not be, as they are widely assumed to be, some species of law or law-like generalisation.

To discuss this issue properly I should have to undertake to examine several important problems in the philosophy of science and this would be out of place in a monograph ostensibly about history. But I hope I have said enough to show that, as I have argued throughout, theoretical and historical explanation are importantly different and a proper grasp of this fact will enable us to escape the difficulty which Hempel has here uncovered.

5. Finally, I should like to point to a congruence of opinion which, though it lends no support to my overall argument, at least shows that what I say bears some relation to the discussion of explanation in general. The logic of explanation in science has, it seems to me, met with more promising treatment in recent years than explanation in history. I have already referred to essays by Alston and Salmon which are notable contributions to this aspect of the philosophy of science. Alston, as we have seen, thinks that explanation in pure science is not concerned with particular facts and argues further that the possession of well-confirmed generalisations in these sciences does not necessarily put us in a position to explain any particular instance. It might be thought that whereas Hempel's model had the virtue of showing the unity of explanation in quite different contexts and hence of giving some underlying unity to the empirical sciences, arguments which purport to detect a radical difference between theoretical and historical explanation leave it quite unclear how they could both be forms of the same thing, explanation. But this need not be so. The main burden of Salmon's recent writings,[11] and in the latest of these he endorses Alston's views, is that theoretical explanation is not a form of argument at all, but that to explain a regularity is to adduce some matter of fact, about the statistical relevance of one phenomenon to another. Similarly, it is an important part of my thesis that historical explanation is not a matter of argument either, but consists rather in the ascertaining of matters of historical fact. This suggests more abstractly that theoretical and historical explanation have some common characteristics and it implies, moreover, that attention to explanation in the pure theoretical sciences no less than historical explanation will show the general structure of explanation ('E', 'C', and 'L') upon which both supporters and opponents of the covering law model have tended to agree, to be mistaken.

For several reasons it seems fitting to end with an *apologia* as well as a summary. If my argument has been sound we have seen how one important philosophical debate about historical explanation has been confounded by radical uncertainty, first about what is involved in qualifying 'explanation' one way rather than another, and secondly over the proper place of appeals to the practice of historians in philosophical argument. On the one hand Hempel and Brodbeck, just because they have a great deal to say about explanation have little or nothing to say about history, and what can be gleaned from their writings or the writings of those who have followed them suggests that they rely upon a dichotomy between history and nature on which their opponents also rest a great deal but which, as a matter of fact, cannot be sustained to the comfort of either party. That history and nature are not diametrically opposed is a conclusion for which I have argued at some length because it is perhaps the single most important claim I advance in this monograph, important not just because the converse has been widely assumed or accepted by philosophers of history, but because it enjoys considerable support in what we might call the common intellectual consciousness of the times. An allied distinction, equally untenable and useless, is that between scientific and historical explanation, which I have argued presents us with no genuine contrast whatever. These are not insubstantial conclusions and have this merit if no other that they replace confusion with some degree of clarity.

But an *apologia* is necessary because it will appear to many that the substance of the conclusions dwindles a good deal once we see *how* these dichotomies have been shown to be false. The problems with which Hempel, Dray and so on were concerned have not so much been solved or even dissolved as sidestepped and a large number of issues left unresolved. For instance, someone could accept all that I say and, despite my invocation of Davidson, still argue about whether explanations involve an ineliminable appeal to generality at some point or other, whether actions can be caused, whether reasons are causes, whether the connections that can be made between the events in a natural history are ultimately different or the same as the connections that may be made between the events of human history, and whether or not historical determinism makes sense. Given that such a large number of the problems which have exercised philosophers of history remain not just unresolved but quite open, it is highly questionable whether the conclusions advanced in this monograph contribute anything to analytical philosophy of history as it has hitherto been understood.

I have been aware of this reservation throughout and have done my best both to rebut some of the ways in which it might be articulated further and to show that it is not entirely just. I do not think that my arguments leave all the customary debates untouched but it must be admitted that part of my strategy has been to insist that for my purposes an answer to many of the questions debated is not needed. Whether or not utter triviality is what results from this strategy I leave readers to judge but its motivation has not been the desire to reach easy solutions to difficult or intractable problems, but rather to insist that for the purposes of the philosophy of history it is the bearing of these problems upon history that must count before all else. If, as I have argued, this bearing is not very great and if, as may well appear to be the case, the philosophical problems that history presents are rather limited, and if, further, all those who have been regarded as philosophers of history have not had any great interest in history so much as explanation, or action, or reason and intelligibility, so that the strictly historical component strikes them as not worth a great deal of attention, this can hardly be a fault on my part. In short, if the philosophy of historical explanation here presented turns out to be true but dull this is still an advance on philosophy of a more exciting kind which, while it is presented as the philosophy of historical explanation, is really about something else. But even this may be to allow too much to critics for I should claim that the mistaken notions about historical explanation I have been examining constitute only one aspect of a more general misunderstanding of the nature of history as a whole.

Notes

1 In this essay I am interested in history and thus take this example. But the *Principles of Art* would do just as well, in many ways better.

2 Of course Wittgenstein did not himself use it in this way, but it seems consonant enough with what he says about metaphysics.

3 This expression is often used to refer to the deductive model only, but I shall use it to refer to Hempel's account of explanation as a whole.

4 I owe this parallel to Christopher Bryant.

5 This is not quite true of Oakeshott. *Experience and its Modes* appeared in 1933 but the essay 'On the Activity of Being an Historian' did not appear till 1962. However, it makes no reference to Hempel.

6 Though as a matter of fact the section from which I have been quoting appeared first in the reasonably polished form of an inaugural lecture.

7 In my elaboration of Ball's view I have relied upon a supplementary paper of his, 'Rational Explanation Revisited', *Proceedings of the Fifth International Congress of Logic, Methodology and Philosophy of Science* (London, Ontario, 1975).

8 See for example Alan Donagan who says about the explanation of the death of Giordano Bruno, 'Here, indeed is an explanation which rests on a law from natural science; but it is not an historical explanation, because Bruno's death, as such, was not an event involving human action', 'The Popper-Hempel Theory Reconsidered', *History and Theory,* vol. 1, p. 15. Again, W B Gallie asserts that 'characteristically historical explanations can be described in the first instance as . . . explanations of the deeds of men (individuals, groups, nations, etc.)', 'Explanations in History and the Genetic Sciences', *Mind* (1955) vol. lxiv, p. 170.

9 It is obvious of course that the generalisations are very interesting in themselves and that we might seek an explanation of these. But since if we did it would be the regularity that interested us the explanation would have to be a theoretical one, as characterised above, and would not be pertinent to the explanation of this particular event.

10 The example is mine but the point is made by A C Danto in his book *Analytical Philosophy of History.* In my view he goes on to draw some erroneous conclusions about the importance of narrative from it.

11 See, for instance, W Salmon, 'Theoretical Explanation' in Körners (ed), *Explanation*.

Bibliography

ESSAYS AND ARTICLES

[1] **Alston, W P,** 'The Explanation of Particular Facts in Science', *Journal of the Philosophy of Science* (1971)

[2] **Ball, T,** 'On "Historical" Explanation', *Philosophy of Social Science,* vol. 2 (1972)

[3] **Ball, T,** 'Rational Explanation Revisited', *Proceedings of the Fifth International Congress of Logic, Methodology and Philosophy of Science* (London, Ontario, 1975)

[4] **Brodbeck, M,** 'Explanation, Prediction and Imperfect Knowledge' in [24]

[5] **Donagan, A,** 'Explanation in History' in [26]

[6] **Donagan, A,** 'The Popper-Hempel Theory Reconsidered', *History and Theory,* vol. 4 (1964)

[7] **Gallie, W B,** *'Explanations in History and the Genetic Sciences'* in [17]

[8] **Hempel, C G,** 'Deductive-Nomological Explanation Versus Statistical Explanation' in [24]

[9] **Hempel, C G,** 'Explanation in Science and in History' in [20]

[10] **Hempel, C G,** 'Reasons and Covering Laws in Historical Explanation' in [29]

[11] **Hempel, C G and Oppenheim, P,** 'Studies in the Logic of Explanation' in [17]

[12] **MacIntyre, A,** 'Is a Science of Comparative Politics Possible?' in [31]

[13] **Oakeshott, M,** 'The Voice of Poetry in the Conversation of Mankind' in [34]

[14] **Salmon, W C,** 'Theoretical Explanation' in Korner, S (ed), *Explanation* (Oxford, 1975)

[15] **Scriven, M,** 'Truisms as the Grounds for Historical Explanations' in [26]

[16] **White, M,** 'Historical Explanation' in [26]

BOOKS

[17] **Brody, B A (ed),** *Readings in the Philosophy of Science* (Englewood Cliffs, N.J., 1970)

[18] **Collingwood, R G,** *The Idea of History* (Oxford, 1946)

[19] **Collingwood, R G,** *Speculum Mentis* (Oxford, 1924)

[20] **Colodny, R,** *Frontiers of Science and Philosophy* (London, 1964)

[21] **Danto, A C,** *Analytical Philosophy of History* (Cambridge, 1965)

[22] Davidson, D, *Actions and Events* (Oxford, 1980)
[23] Dray, W H, *Laws and Explanations in History* (Oxford, 1952)
[24] Feigl and Maxwell (eds), *Minnesota Studies in the Philosophy of Science* III (Minnesota, 1962)
[25] Gardiner, P, *The Nature of Historical Explanation* (Oxford, 1952)
[26] Gardiner, P (ed), *Theories of History* (New York, 1959)
[27] Goodman, N, *Fact, Fiction and Forecast* (London, 1954)
[28] Hempel, C G, *Aspects of Scientific Explanation* (New York, 1965)
[29] Hook, S (ed), *Philosophy of History* (New York, 1963)
[30] Kuhn, T S, *The Structure of Scientific Revolutions* (Chicago, 1962)
[31] MacIntyre, A, *Against the Self-Images of the Age* (London, 1971)
[32] Nozick, R, *Anarchy, State and Utopia* (Oxford, 1971)
[33] Oakeshott, M, *Experience and its Modes* (Cambridge, 1933)
[34] Oakeshott, M, *Rationalism in Politics and Other Essays* (London, 1962)
[35] Popper, K, *The Open Society and its Enemies* (London, 1945)
[36] Popper, K, *The Poverty of Historicism* (London, 1961)
[37] Rawls, J, *A Theory of Justice* (Oxford, 1972)
[38] Salmon, W C, *Statistical Explanation and Statistical Relevance* (Pittsburgh, 1971)
[39] White, M, *Foundations of Historical Knowledge* (New York, 1965)
[40] Winks, R (ed), *Historians and Evidence* (New York, 1968)
[41] Wittgenstein, L, *Philosophical Investigations*, 3rd edn (Oxford, 1967)